GO, SET THE WORLD ON FIRE
A New Evangelisation

Fr Ken Barker

Modotti Press
"Where religion does matter"

Published in 2018 by Connor Court Publishing Pty Ltd

Copyright © Fr Ken Barker MGL 2018

ALL RIGHTS RESERVED. This book contains material protected under International and Federal Copyright Laws and Treaties. Any unauthorised reprint or use of this material is prohibited. No part of this book may be reproduced or transmitted in any form or by any means, electronic or mechanical, including photocopying, recording, or by any information storage and retrieval system without express written permission from the publisher.

Nihil Obstat
Rev Warrick G. Tonkin BA, DipEd, BTh, MEd.
Most Rev Christopher Prowse DD STD
Archbishop of Canberra and Goulburn

Modotti Press (An imprint of Connor Court Publishing).
PO Box 7257
Redland Bay QLD 4165
sales@connorcourt.com
www.connorcourt.com

ISBN: 9781925501933

Front cover design: Lawrence Yuen MGL

Bible quotations from the New Revised Standard Version Bible
Printed in Australia

CONTENTS

FOREWORD... v

INTRODUCTION: OUR PURPOSE......................... ix

1: WHY EVANGELISE?... 1

2: A NEW EVAGELISATION.. 9

3: A NEW PENTECOST.. 21

4: GIFTS OF THE SPIRIT.. 35

5: CHALLENGES WE FACE.. 45

6: WITNESS OF LIFE.. 57

7: PROCLAIMING THE KERYGMA............................... 67

8: GRACE AND MERCY.. 79

9: A PROCESS OF CONVERSION................................... 87

10: THE GIFT OF PREACHING...................................... 97

11: THE GIFT OF HEALING..109

12: A COMMUNITY OF DISCIPLES ON MISSION.....127

13: PRIORITY OF THE POOR... 139

14: NEW EXPRESSIONS AND METHOD..................... 147

15: THE POWER OF INTERCESSION..........................161

16: THE EVANGELISERS..175

ENDNOTES..191

I want to especially express my gratitude to Selina Hasham for working on the text in preparation for publication. Also thanks to Lawrence Yuen MGL who designed such a beautiful cover. I am particularly thankful for all the MGL brothers with whom I live. They have been very supportive and patient with me. I am dedicating this book to St John Paul II who first called for a new evangelisation, and is now interceding that we will realise his vision in our day.

FOREWORD

It has been over fifty years now since the Charismatic Renewal has entered the Catholic Church.

In the earlier years the introduction of essential features of the Charismatic Renewal came as quite a surprise for Catholics. The listening to the personal testimonies of the faith lives of people, the clapping and holding upwards of the hands, the term and explanation of the "Baptism of the Holy Spirit", the exercise of the charismatic gifts in community, extra attentiveness to the reading of the scriptures and celebration of the Sacraments, its ecumenical dimension, the increased thirst for prayer and service to the poor, and so on, all seemed rather exotic to the uninitiated.

Fifty years later, it seems that these features of the Charismatic Renewal are now more than ever commonplace in the life of the Church

This was on display as never before when over 50,000 people accepted the invitation of Pope Francis to join him in a charismatic rally at Rome's Circus Maximus on Pentecost 2017.

I was present. It felt as if something truly historic was taking place. This was evident to me in the fact that the Pope was hosting an ecumenical charismatic prayer rally. For a generous part of this time together with people from all around the world the Pope seemed to be co-hosting the gathering with a Pentecostal Pastor of international repute.

It has not been long since Catholics and Pentecostals had very little to do with each other. Over the years there has been some nasty name-calling and efforts to distance each other in theology and prayer. Not anymore! This is surely a subtle "ecumenical grace" of some importance! Come Holy Spirit!

In this easy to read book of Fr Ken Barker, the Founder and Moderator of the Missionaries of God's Love, offers a thorough appraisal of the gifts of the Charismatic Renewal to the wider Church over these last fifty years. These gifts are at the service of the Church's missionary mandate.

In "Go, Set the World on Fire – a new evangelisation", Fr Barker aims to articulate the "fundamental principles of the new evangelisation needed in the Church today."

There are most helpful short explanations of the meaning and importance of the charisms, the kerygma, healing, dialogue, intercession and the qualities most needed today for the evangelists of the new evangelisation.

The term "new evangelisation" was first coined by St Pope John Paul II and popularised further by Pope Benedict XVI. Pope Francis accepts the term but expands it further and seems to prefer the expression "missionary discipleship". Fr Barker explains the development of this important missionary term and draws out its importance in our world today.

I commend to you this comprehensive explanation of current Catholic teaching on evangelisation.

As Fr Ken Barker, a great Catholic evangelist himself, unambiguously states: "our mission is to set the world on fire with the love of God."

Archbishop Christopher Prowse
Catholic Archbishop of Canberra and Goulburn

"All authority in heaven and on earth has been given to me. Go, therefore, make disciples of all the nations; baptise them in the name of the Father and of the Son and of the Holy Spirit, and teach them to observe all the commands I gave you. And know that I am with you always; yes, to the end of time." Mt 28:18-20

INTRODUCTION
OUR PURPOSE

Our mission is to set the world on fire with the love of God. Nothing is more important than this. The human person needs many things to live a fulfilled life; but nothing is more urgent than knowing God's love. We are made for the love of God and our hearts are empty and hungry until we experience his love.

When in the 16th century Ignatius Loyola sent out the first "companions of Jesus", now known as the Jesuits, he is reported to have commissioned them with the words, "Go, set all afire". That injunction succinctly sums up the task the Lord has given us today. During his earthly ministry Jesus exclaimed, "I have come to bring fire to the earth and how I wish it were blazing already!" (Lk 12:49). This was his deepest desire; that the love of God burning in his heart would be given to all. But Jesus knew this was not possible until he underwent his own "baptism of fire" in his passion and death on the cross. On Calvary his burning love for all men and women was manifest. It was the culmination of three years of Spirit-filled ministry, blazing with love for all whom he met. This sacrificial love took him to the cross for our sake. He knew this was the only way the fire of God's love could come to all men and women.

True to his promise, when Jesus rose from the dead and returned to the Father, the Holy Spirit was poured out upon the world at Pentecost. Fire to the earth! Our mission is to spread this fire of the Spirit, which flows from the heart of Jesus crucified and risen. To catch this fire is to know the saving power of Jesus and to be filled with the Holy Spirit. It is to be set on fire with love for God and a passion for the kingdom. When this love of God fills our hearts nothing can restrain us from sharing this gift with others. Jesus becomes the joy of our lives and we want to proclaim this good news to all.

This is our fundamental identity as Church. This is why we exist. This is our deepest purpose; to share the love of God with others. How much we need to discover who we are! As Catherine of Siena said, "Become who God wants you to be and you will set the world on fire!" What does God want us to be? The people who know his love, the people who have so fallen in love with him that we want only to do his will. As Jesus said, "My food is to do the will of the one who sent me" (Jn 4:34). The will of the Father is that all men and women be brought to salvation by coming to know the redeeming love of Jesus. Once our hearts are captured by the love of God our concern is no longer for ourselves, but for others. We then have a passionate desire to bring the gift of God's love revealed in Jesus to all men and women.

God's purpose is to bring every man and woman on the face of the earth to know his saving love in Jesus Christ. He has established a wonderfully effective instrument to fulfil this purpose – the Church. This is why the Church exists. As Pope Paul VI reminded us, "the essence of the Church is to evangelise, this is its deepest purpose".[1] This sort of bald statement can raise shackles in the hearts of some who instinctively cry, "triumphalism!" Didn't Vatican II make it clear that people can be saved outside the Church if they live according to the revelation given them and remain faithful to their conscience? Yes, true, but it is not helpful to define an entity by something written in the brackets. It would be like an international company which builds submarines defining itself in terms of sonar systems to prevent collisions with whales. No doubt an important issue to have in brackets, but not at the core of their mission! Coming back to the Church, our core mission is the proclamation of the good news of Jesus Christ for the salvation of all. Certainly we can mention in brackets that it is possible for people to gain salvation without explicitly knowing Christ and his Church. That is good "brackets theology", but it should not distract us from our core mission.

Is this triumphalistic? No! The "triumphalism" challenged at Vatican II was the blithe assumption that the Church was moving through history totally free of mistakes, without any faults, gloriously right in every sphere of knowledge or human undertaking. This thinking was smashed by the Council. We witnessed the moving outcome of this shift in mind-set when Pope John Paul II in the Jubilee Year 2000 publicly repented before the world for the past sins of the Church. To claim that the Church is the harbinger of good news to all men and women, and the privileged means of their salvation, is not to be triumphalist at all. Salvation is sheer gift from God. More than ever we are aware that we are a wounded Church, a manifest bunch of sinners, merely "earthenware vessels" holding the treasure of Christ "to make it clear that such and overwhelming power comes from God and not from us" (2Cor 4:7).

While we eschew any hint of "triumphalism" we are nevertheless meant to have deep faith in the victory of Christ over all evil. Possibly this affirmation of faith is a challenge to many of us. The deepest crisis in the Church today is not the pressures upon us from the world at large, such as secularism, relativism, atheism, scientism, or whatever other "ism" we may want to name. Rather there is a root problem in the minds and hearts of Church adherents themselves, a crisis of faith. The problem is not foremost with the unbelieving world, and the threat it poses to the Church, but rather with those of us who profess belief, but don't believe enough! John tells us, "This is the victory over the world – our faith. Who can overcome the world? Only the one who believes that Jesus is the Son of God" (1Jn 5:4-5).

How much do I really believe God has sent his Son, Jesus Christ, into the world to save the world? Do I believe that the Holy Spirit is active already in the lives of those whom I encounter? Do I believe that God could use me to influence the lives of others towards his kingdom? Evangelisation is not our work. Rather it is God's work accomplished through us. But we need to believe this. To loosely quote St Augustine, "God who created us without our cooperation will not redeem us without our cooperation". God needs us to say "yes" with a deep response of faith to be his instruments in the work of evangelisation. Paul VI pointed out that the Holy Spirit is "the principal agent of evangelisation"[2]. So it is not all up to us. We can happily let go of any "Messiah complex", thinking we must do the work alone. But just as importantly, we need to avoid falling into a sense of failure and resignation as we face the current hostility against the Church. The answer is rather to join the apostles and pray for an increase in faith! "Lord, increase our faith!" We need the sort of faith that Jesus spoke about – expectant faith that moves mountains, even if our faith is only the size of a mustard seed.

Do I really believe that Jesus' promise is true that "the gates of hell will not prevail" against the Church? Maybe first we need to understand the promise. Jesus is not saying we will be protected from human enemies railing against the Church and persecuting those who seek to bring the good news. Rather it is a promise that we have nothing to fear from any hatred and hostility. We are to rejoice when persecuted because this will surely bring the good fruit of conversions. As Tertullian famously said, "The blood of martyrs is the seed of Christians". Jesus' promise is that if the Church is fulfilling its purpose in the world, faithfully proclaiming the good news, the strongholds of Satan in the hearts and minds of people will be overcome and the truth made manifest. We must believe this. The greatest protection for the Church today is not to become defensive by "circling the wagons" ready to fight until the death. Rather we are meant to be on the offensive with the way of love and the word of God as the sword of the Spirit, shod with shoes eager to spread the good news of the gospel of peace. As Isaiah says, "the footsteps of those who proclaim the good news of peace is a welcome sound" (Is 52:7).

In this book I want to enunciate some of the fundamental principles of the new evangelisation needed in the Church today. I trust it will help you form your vision for the renewal of the Church's missionary thrust, and inspire us all to go forward confidently as a community of missionary disciples. I am not aiming to cover the whole range of topics possible. Rather I intend to focus on what I consider most vital for our mission and most urgent for this time in the Church's history. The reader would not necessarily need to start at the beginning, but could dive into a later chapter that attracts immediate attention. Some sections will be more personally interesting than others. However, I would urge you to make your way through the whole text at some time, since I am convinced that all the principles mentioned here are necessary. Each topic on its own will be useful, but all together they make an explosive recipe for change and restoration. In the 13th century Francis of Assisi heard the words from the cross of Jesus, "Go, rebuild my Church". I trust these pages will help you to hear the Lord's agenda for rebuilding his Church in the 21st century. The same Holy Spirit who inspired Francis is energising the Church again with a new evangelisation. It is time to seize the moment of grace.

1
WHY EVANGELISE?

Before describing the new evangelisation let's plumb more deeply why we would bother proclaiming the good news. What are our motives?

People Need Jesus

The *first reason* is simply that people need Jesus! He is the answer to the deepest questions and desires of the human heart. So many people suffer with an inner emptiness even though their lives are full of activities, sensate stimulation and sensual pleasure. Underneath this veneer there is an ache for "more". Within the hearts of many there is a hidden exasperation: "there must be more than this!" We Christians offer the "more" that hearts hunger for, the rich experience of the saving love of God in Jesus Christ. So many have little meaning or purpose to their lives; the so-called "good times" only take one so far. Again and again we witness celebrities who supposedly "have it all" – money, fame, success, opulent life-style – but at the end of the day they are desperately lonely, longing for meaningful relationship and a sense of purpose in the universe. A living relationship with the Risen Jesus brings a clear understanding of the meaning of life and a clear direction towards where we are ultimately headed. It brings lasting hope.

Many are still seeking personal identity – who am I? Do I have worth? Where is my security? Am I significant? Only a personal encounter with Jesus and an awareness of being a new creation as a son or daughter of God can fully meet this need. We discover who we really are not by looking at ourselves, but by looking to Christ, and through him to the loving Father he came to reveal. It is such a liberation to experience oneself in the light of God's loving gaze upon us. Jesus is the great "I am" in whom we find our identity. Many suffer also from a lack of connectedness due to relational breakdown within family of origin or amongst friendship circles or in marriage. Relational fracture is rife in today's society and the needed healing can only be ultimately found in Christ, who has come to reconcile and bring lasting peace. His gift of forgiveness from the cross makes it possible to break the cycle of violence in our relationships by genuine forgiveness and reconciliation.

The Heart of Jesus for the Lost

The *second reason* is closely connected to the first. We share the compassionate heart of Jesus for the lost. We want people to experience the new life he came to bring: "I have come that you may have life and have it to the full" (Jn 10:10). Out of love for others we want to share who Jesus is for us; we want to have them experience his impact in their lives as we have experienced it. We want to share the infinite treasure of Christ as the most precious gift we can bring. Sometimes people say, "You Christians who preach the gospel are imposing your beliefs on others". But we are not imposing, but *proposing*. We are offering a precious gift which, if it is accepted, really sets people free. People have a right to know the truth. As Jesus said, "If you make my word your home you will indeed be my disciples; you will know the truth and the truth will set you free" (Jn 8:31-32).

Jesus is the Truth

This brings us to *the third reason* which is that Jesus *is* the truth. Of course in the relativism of today's society people become uncomfortable when Christians claim to have the truth. They would rather believe that each person has their own truth, so it is best just to tolerate one another in our differences. Tolerance is a great virtue, but it should never compromise the truth. People are inclined to say, "It does not matter what you believe so long as you are sincere". But the trouble is that people can be sincerely wrong. Adolf Hitler sincerely believed in his Nazi ideology. But he was absolutely wrong. God is the author of truth not us. We proclaim certain doctrines and moral teachings to be true because they are revealed by God. But, more than that, we proclaim "Jesus is the truth". By this we mean that we have personally experienced the reality of Christ and in doing so we perceive the world around us differently. This whole new way of seeing things through the eyes of faith makes all the difference for good human living.

Need to be Saved

A *fourth reason* is that we all need to be saved from sin and find new life. There is endless conflict and trouble in the world, and at the deepest level there is the problem of sin. Unfortunately, we are prone to turn away from God and turn towards creatures. This means we turn created realities into idols – money, alcohol, sex, success, shopping or whatever. We are also inclined to be fundamentally self-centred and thus push God to the periphery of our lives. This always bears bad fruit. We tend to be disobedient to God's will preferring to do things our own way and following our own selfish desires. No one but Jesus can save us from sin. That is why he came.

The human race feverishly tries all sorts of ventures to save ourselves. Some think that science and technology will save us. Others tend to think that education will save us. Others think that social engineering and politics will save us. But all of these human efforts, as good as they are, fall far short of meeting the problem. It can be likened to rearranging the chairs on the deck of the Titanic after it hit the iceberg. All those efforts are delusional if we feel they are solving the ultimate problem. The real issue is that there is a gaping hole in the hull of the ship. For the human race this is called sin. It has been dealt with by Jesus when, as our Saviour, he hung on the cross for us and rose from the dead. But we need to open our hearts to receive this saving grace won for us by Jesus.

When Jesus came to the synagogue at Nazareth he took the scroll of the prophet Isaiah and read, "The spirit of the Lord is upon me, because he has anointed me to bring good news to the poor" (Lk 4:18). He was proclaiming his reason for coming into the world – to set the captives free, to break the chains that bind us up, to save us from the blindness of sin and give us new sight, to rescue us from the paralysis of spirit caused by sin, to bring the good news to all who are open to receive his liberating power. The fundamental bondage which holds us all captive, at least to some degree, is sin. To overlook this reality is to live in illusion. As John says, "If we say we have no sin in us, we are deceiving ourselves and refusing to accept the truth" (1Jn 1:8). God who is light has come to bring us out of this darkness.

To Show People the Way to Heaven

A *fifth reason* is that we want to show people the way to heaven. The Curé of Ars, Jean Vianney, lost his way when he was walking through the French countryside to take up his new priestly appointment. He met a young man and promised, "You show me the way to Ars, and I will show you the way to heaven". That is our purpose; to lead people to God, to accompany them on this earthly pilgrimage as they move forward to their ultimate home in heaven. They need to discover that God has already come to us and dwells within us from baptism. To the extent that we open ourselves to him we begin already to experience heaven in our souls. Paul says, "For all who are in Christ there is a new creation; the old is gone and the new is here" (2Cor 5:17). He creates a longing in our hearts for total union with him. The love of God is like a magnet. He wins the soul by gentle persuasion and draws us more and more into a heart to heart relationship with him. Our proclamation of the gospel is meant to be contagious. We do not "proselytise" which suggests manipulation or coercion or in some way to trick people into becoming a Christian. We seek to attract others by the lives we live and the message we preach. God is always drawing the human heart to himself. We are simply his mouth, his hands, and his feet.

Connected to the fifth reason is the flip side of this decision for heaven. We are designed with a fundamental orientation towards heaven. If we don't make decisions that lead us to heaven, we could end up eternally lost. God takes our free will so seriously that we can shut ourselves out from the salvation won for us by Jesus. We know, as I said earlier, that it's possible for someone to be saved without knowing Jesus, but we also know the only water-tight guarantee of salvation is through faith and baptism lived well. We don't want anyone to lose the opportunity for eternal bliss with God forever. Jesus once gave a significant warning that none of us can afford to ignore: "Enter through the narrow gate, for the road is wide and easy that leads to destruction, and many take it. For the gate is narrow and the road is hard that leads to life, and there are few who take it" (Mt 7:13). Our decisions now have eternal repercussions. Evangelisation is helping one another make decisions in response to God's saving love that bide well for eternity.

To Change the World

A *sixth reason* to evangelise is because we love this world and we want to see it change for the better. We know that the world will only change if human hearts change. We want a world governed by the Beatitudes of Christ, a whole new way of living. But this can only happen when genuine conversion happens. In a world where increasing numbers of displaced people are refugees, human trafficking and the narcotics trade are rife, the abuse and exploitation of minors continues, all sorts of corruption and criminal activity occur, and the lives of many are pushed to the fringes of society, neglected and left to fend for themselves, the proclamation of the gospel which affirms the dignity of each human person is urgent indeed. We want our evangelising to transform the culture of modern society so that we can build a new "civilisation of life and love".

Jesus Told Us to Do It

A *seventh reason* to evangelise is because Jesus commanded us to do so. We are simply obeying his command. The word "go" appears 233 times in the New Testament and 54 times in Matthew's gospel. Jesus tells us to "go". "Go to the lost sheep", "Go and tell John", "Go and invite all you meet", "Go and make disciples". Clearly we are to go and make a difference in the lives of others through the good news we preach, making disciples and being with the poor. Jesus said to the first apostles, "As the Father has sent me, so I am sending you" (Jn 20:21). We cannot ignore this desire of Jesus to send us to share in his mission in the world. It is both a great privilege and a demanding responsibility.

When Jesus called his first disciples he simply said, "Follow me and I will make you fishers of people" (Mk 1:17). Our purpose is to fish for people, to bring others to Jesus. A parable can help us reflect on this. Once upon a time there was a fishing clubhouse built close to a large lake full of many varieties of fish. People loved to be part of this fishing club. There were large auditoriums for having conferences about fishing, audio-visual equipment for showing fishing films and videos, lots of seminars on the art of fishing, weekly celebrations of fishing, and on special days they remembered the great fishermen of old. They were very well stocked with all the gear necessary for fishing. They had some exciting displays of rods, lines, tackle and various lures used to catch fish. But there was one thing odd about this fishing club. No one ever actually went fishing! There were fishing songs, fishing dramas, fishing movies. But no one went fishing!

Then one day, a young man was so inspired by a fishing movie he actually got together a fishing rod and some bait, and ventured out to the lake nearby. He threw out his line and immediately caught this big fish. He landed it safely, and came back to the club to show off his catch. Well, everyone was so excited. Someone had actually caught a fish. They had a whole week of celebrations as they feted their new hero. In fact they decided to bestow on him the greatest honour – the millennium medal for fishing! They thought his feat was so extraordinary that they decided to send him overseas to study fishology. So after a number of years he returned with a PhD in fishology, and then toured the nation lecturing on the theory and practice of fishing. But, you know what? He never went fishing again!

In the Church today we do a lot of talking and writing about fishing, like this present book. But who is actually *doing* some fishing? Some time ago we had a conference on evangelisation. At the end of the week, during a final prayer meeting, a woman stood up to give a prophecy. To our surprise she simply sang loudly, "Gone fishin'!", and sat down. We were embarrassed by this rather odd behaviour. But afterwards I thought to myself, "Maybe it *was* a prophecy". It occurred to me that if all the people at their desks in Church bureaucracies around the country, and all those leaders, like me at the moment , who are sitting at their computers, could just for at least one day a week put a sign on their doors, "Gone fishin'!", we would be a healthier Church!

2
A NEW EVANGELISATION

The term "evangelisation" is still finding its way into the vocabulary of the Catholic people at large, but it certainly has strong currency now amongst clergy and the more committed laity. It has become the ecclesial "buzz" word. We know that we ought to be about evangelisation, but there's a large variety of interpretations of what this really means. So-called evangelising programs may be aimed at gaining new members by invitations to Church clubs, societies or social activities, or by attracting people back to Sunday attendance. As good as these sort of programs are, we cannot yet claim them as "evangelisation" as such. Evangelisation does not just aim at gaining church adherence, but at bringing people to conversion to Christ. The priority is on a personal encounter with the Risen Jesus. Pope Paul VI put it plainly,

> Evangelisation will always contain – as the foundation, centre, and at the same time, summit of its dynamism – a clear proclamation that, in Jesus Christ, the Son of God made man, who died and rose from the dead, salvation is offered to all, as a gift of God's grace and mercy.[3]

Sometimes Catholics can consider this emphasis on the proclamation of Christ as sounding more Protestant in flavour than genuinely Catholic. This is because it is overtly evangelical; the sort of thing which we associate with Protestant televangelists. Yet the recent Popes themselves have urged us in this direction. Without this core proclamation of Christ, aimed towards personal conversion to him as one's Saviour and Lord, evangelisation is emptied of its true meaning. Pope John Paul II put it succinctly,

> The proclamation of the Word of God has Christian conversion as its aim: a complete and sincere adherence to Christ and his gospel through faith….Conversion means accepting, by a personal decision, the saving sovereignty of Christ and becoming his disciple.[4]

The key to our Christian life is that we encounter ever more deeply the saving love of Jesus who died for our sins and rose for our justification. We need to know the joy flowing from the infinite love of God which we encounter in Jesus Christ. As Benedict XVI declared, "Being a Christian is not the result of an ethical choice or a lofty idea, but the encounter with an event, a person, which gives life a new horizon and a decisive direction".[5] This means that many practising Catholics need to be evangelised before they can become evangelists. Indeed, we all need to be evangelised again and again. No matter how long we have been on the journey of discipleship we all need to be born anew in the joy of a deeper relationship with Christ.

Focus on the Essentials

Our ecclesial ministries are seriously lacking if we only provide doctrinal teaching, moral instruction, liturgical initiation, and church membership, without the proclamation of the good news of Jesus at the heart of this endeavour. Pope Francis says, "The message has to concentrate on the essentials, on what is most beautiful, most grand, most appealing and at the same time most necessary"[6]. He urges us to simplify the message by concentrating on the basic core, so that "what shines forth is the beauty of the saving love of God made manifest in Jesus Christ who died and rose from the dead"[7]. Pope

Francis is urging us to start from Christ. He is speaking from his own pastoral experience. He wants to combat a minimalist Catholicism which is "reduced to mere baggage, to a collection of rules and prohibitions, to fragmented devotional practices, to selective and partial adherence to the truths of the faith, to occasional participation in some sacraments, to the repetition of doctrinal principles, to bland or nervous moralising, that does not convert the life of the baptised." [8] He knows that nominal Catholicism will not stand before the testing trials of our present age. The bishops of Latin America put the issue poignantly:

> Here lies the fundamental challenge that we face: to show the Church's capacity to promote and form disciples and missionaries who respond to the calling received and to communicate everywhere, in an outpouring of gratitude and joy, the gift of the encounter with Jesus Christ. We have no other treasure but that. We have no other happiness, no other priority, but to be instruments of the Spirit of God, as Church, so that Jesus Christ may be known, followed, loved, adored, announced, and communicated to all, despite difficulties and resistances. This is the best service – his service – that the Church has to offer people and nations.[9]

What is the New Evangelisation?

The term has a history. It was coined first by Pope John Paul II when speaking to the Latin American bishops in 1983 in Haiti and used often by him after this. He emphasised it was not a new gospel as such but new in "ardour, methods, and expressions".[10] He defined it primarily as a new effort of evangelisation directed not only to traditional "mission territories" but especially to regions of traditional Christian cultural backgrounds "where entire groups of the baptised have lost a living sense of the faith, or even no longer consider themselves members of the Church, and live a life far removed from Christ and his gospel"[11] He was looking for a new evangelising thrust especially in regions such as United States, Australia and Europe where there has been a "tsunami of secularism", causing significant loss of faith and large scale abandonment of the Church. He was also aware that in many areas where the Catholic presence is relatively new, the faith is still shallow. The first missionaries had focused on planting church structures, education, and social welfare. They gained a level of church allegiance which did not sufficiently focus on a profound personal conversion to Christ.

Pope Benedict XVI enthusiastically continued the call of his predecessor and made the extraordinary step of establishing a Pontifical Council for New Evangelisation. He gave the Council the specific task of:

> promoting a renewed evangelisation in countries where the first proclamation of the faith already resounded, and where Churches are present of ancient foundation, but which are going through a progressive secularisation of society and a sort of 'eclipse of the sense of God', which constitutes a challenge to find the appropriate means to propose again the perennial truth of the gospel of Christ.[12]

While papal documents endorsed this new evangelisation it was in fact spearheaded by new lay movements and ecclesial communities that have sprung up spontaneously since the Second Vatican Council. In 1985 Cardinal Ratzinger, before becoming Pope, when reflecting on the crisis in the Church after the Council, saw great hope in these new movements:

> What is hopeful at the level of the universal Church – and that is happening right in the heart of the crisis of the Church in the Western world – is the rise of new movements which

nobody has called into being, but which have sprung spontaneously from the inner vitality of the faith itself. What is manifested in them…is something like a Pentecostal season in the Church. I am thinking, say, of the Charismatic movement, of the Cursillos, of the movement of the Focolare, of the neo-catechumenal communities, of Communion and Liberation, etc.[13]

The Rise of the Laity

This unexpected advent of the new movements underlines a major feature of the new evangelisation. It is new because it is not being driven by the so-called specialists, the priests and religious, but by lay people inspired by the Holy Spirit. It is a return to the initial thrust of evangelising energy birthed at Pentecost. The Acts of the Apostles describes how the initial Pentecost experience launched the powerful apostolic preaching of the gospel, birthing the Church in many centres within the Roman Empire, which was largely a hostile environment for the faith to be planted. From the earliest days and into the post-apostolic era all the people of God belonging to any Christian community were joyfully and courageously preaching the gospel. Lay people, not only the consecrated leaders, took responsibility for this primary task of the Church. Now in the twenty first century, under the grace of a new Pentecost, we are experiencing a resurgence of this evangelising power of the laity.

Throughout the history of the Church there have been different eras when a new surge of the Holy Spirit brought a new energy for proclaiming the good news. Usually these new movements arose at a time of crisis, when it seemed that due to outside pressures the Church was losing its edge and in danger of failing in its mission. In the fourth century, after the Peace of Constantine, the Church was in danger of compromise. Becoming a Christian offered social position and prestige in the Empire. The original desire for holiness and fire to evangelise was dampened. Consequently, the Holy Spirit inspired a young man, Anthony of Egypt, to leave everything and seek God alone in the desert. Others joined him, and what started as a group of hermits eventually became a movement of monastic communities bringing a new fervour and renewal to the whole Church.

In the thirteenth century, when the official Church had become unhealthily wedded to the rich and ruling class, the Holy Spirit inspired Francis of Assisi and Dominic Guzman to embrace evangelical poverty and initiate a movement of mendicant Friars, which again brought new energy and enthusiasm for living the gospel and proclaiming the good news. Again in the sixteenth century, when the Church was fractured by the Reformation, suffering from damaging infighting, the Holy Spirit inspired Ignatius Loyola and his fellow companions to take the good news to the "new world" which was opening in the Americas. Later in the nineteenth century, when the monasteries and religious houses had been closed down in France and it seemed a whole generation was lost to the Church, the Holy Spirit moved sovereignly to raise up out of the ashes a new wave of missionary religious to take the good news to Oceania, and many other regions of the world.

Now in the latter part of the twentieth century and the early stages of the twenty first century, the Church has found itself in crisis again. Faith is suffering from secularism, and indifferentism. The truth is being clouded by what Pope Benedict XVI called a "dictatorship of relativism". On top of these broad cultural influences the Church is embroiled in the sexual abuse scandals, which have rocked her to the core, and caused many to lose confidence in her credibility. At this time of crisis the Holy Spirit is again being poured out abundantly. This time it is not primarily with the monks, or with the friars, or the missionary priests and religious, but with the lay faithful. Across the Christian world there is an unprecedented surge of energy and enthusiasm generated by the experience of a "new Pentecost". The Holy Spirit is still with the Church!!

Missionary Disciples

In a prophetic document ushering in the new millennium Pope John Paul II spoke of the current change in circumstances in the world today: "Even in countries evangelised many centuries ago, the reality of a 'Christian society' is now gone". He was aware that we face a new situation which requires a new evangelisation with a new fire to preach the gospel. He called for this zeal to be in the hearts of all of God's people.

> This passion will not fail to stir in the Church a new sense of mission, which cannot be left to a group of 'specialists' but must involve the responsibility of all the members of the People of God. Those who have come into contact with Christ cannot keep him to themselves, they must proclaim him. A new apostolic outreach is needed, which will be lived as *the everyday commitment of Christian communities and groups*.[14]

Pope Francis agrees entirely with his predecessor, and reminds all the baptised that by virtue of baptism they are "missionary disciples". Every member of God's faithful people "whatever their position in the Church or their level of instruction in the faith, are agents of evangelisation". He insists:

> It would be insufficient to envisage a plan of evangelisation to be carried out by professionals while the rest of the faithful would simply be passive recipients. The new evangelisation calls for personal involvement on the part of each of the baptised.[15]

Pope Francis insists that people do not need a lengthy time of training to become evangelisers. Once we have encountered the love of God in Jesus Christ we have enough qualification to get started. He encourages us not to classify people in the church as either "disciples" or "missionaries". Rather we are all *"missionary* disciples". That is the only type of genuine disciple there is. He reminds us of Andrew who after spending a day with Jesus immediately went to his brother Peter and declared, "We have found the Messiah" (Jn 1:41). The Samaritan woman, after her encounter with Jesus, immediately rushed off to tell her town's folk. We are told many came to believe him "because of the woman's testimony" (Jn 4:39). Also Paul, after his encounter of the Risen Jesus on the road to Damascus "immediately proclaimed Jesus" (Acts 9:20). When we have fallen in love with Jesus, how could we keep such good news to ourselves? As Pope Francis says,

> All of us are called to offer others an explicit witness to the saving love of the Lord, who despite our imperfections offers us his closeness, his word and his strength, and gives meaning to our lives.[16]

This engagement of all the baptised in the Church's mission is the most exciting dimension of *newness* to evangelisation in our times. It is recapturing the dynamism of our origins.

As in the Early Church

In the early Church the missionary task was incumbent on every member. There were some, like the apostles and elders, permanently engaged in evangelisation. But in addition to these the whole community of Christians announced the good news to those around them. They did this spontaneously in their daily lives. It wasn't so much a strategy or tactic, but done quite naturally on the basis of relationships they had with relatives, friends, and co-workers, each according to their charism. Origen (ca 180AD) reports how a pagan, Celsus, somewhat cynically described the evangelical activity of the Christian laity:

> In private houses also we see wool-workers, cobblers, laundry-workers, and the most illiterate and bucolic yokels, who would not dare to say anything at all in front of their elders and more intelligent masters. But whenever they get hold of children in private and some stupid women with them, they let out some astounding statements….they alone, they say, know the right way to live…if they like, they should leave father and their schoolmasters, and go along with the women and little children who are playfellows to the wool dresser's shop, or to the cobbler's or the washerwoman's shop, and they may learn perfection. And by saying this they persuade them.[17]

Since Vatican II the lay apostolate in the Church has often been interpreted in a limited way, not yet capturing the full significance of this moment of grace. The call has been for "power sharing" of roles which are not directly evangelistic. Lay people are called to become "active" within the Church by enlisting as ministers of Holy Communion, joining parish councils, serving on committees etc. All of this is good, but the Holy Spirit is doing more. The role of the laity is not just to help out the clergy in intra-ecclesial activities. This limited way of thinking fails to appreciate that we have entered into a new era in the Church where there is a new awareness of the anointing of "power from on high" on every baptised Christian for the proclamation of the good news. This gift of the Spirit was given especially at Confirmation. The evangelising lay movements have become the vanguard of this radically new way of thinking. Now is the time for *all* the laity to rise up with fresh vision and eagerness for the new evangelisation.

The Importance of Direct Proclamation

Also since Vatican II there has rightly been a strong emphasis on the laity having their apostolate primarily in the secular sphere. But this has often been interpreted exclusively as a "leaven in the midst" within the socio-cultural and political spheres, or as being a genuine witness of a virtuous life. While both involvement in the socio-political arena and the witness of a good life are very important, it would be wrong to eliminate from this perspective the priority of direct proclamation of the good news of Jesus. The secular environments where lay people find themselves are already a field ready for the harvest. Lay people have the privilege of being in spheres of influence not available to the clergy. By witness of their lives and proclamation of the word they can bring many to come to know Christ and give their lives over to his love. Pope John Paul II put out the call:

> The lay faithful, precisely because they are members of the Church, have the vocation and mission of proclaiming the gospel: they are prepared for this work by the sacraments of Christian initiation and by the gifts of the Holy Spirit.[18]

In this context of strongly encouraging the laity to evangelise, Pope John Paul II quoted his predecessor Pope Paul VI: "To evangelise is the grace and vocation proper to the Church, her most profound identity".[19] By "Church" he does not mean the official office-bearers of the Church, but the whole body, all the members together in one great act of witness to the love of God and proclamation of God's good news to all. Pope Francis urges us to form truly evangelising communities of missionary disciples:

An evangelising community knows that the Lord has taken the initiative, he has loved us first (cf. 1Jn 4:19), and therefore we can move forward, boldly take the initiative, go out to others, seek those who have fallen away, stand at the crossroads and welcome the outcast.[20]

So it is ultimately not healthy for us to focus on tensions between the clerical and lay contributions to the work of evangelisation, as if they are in competition with one another. Rather it is a matter of becoming a genuine community with all states of life working together with their different charisms to participate in the mission of Jesus himself to bring the lost into communion with him. This is the work of a community which witnesses to the beliefs, values, and way of life of the kingdom of God and joyfully proclaims the good news of Jesus to those around them.

3
A NEW PENTECOST

Evangelising in the Power of the Spirit

To be effective the "new evangelisation" needs to be done under the power of the Holy Spirit. All our efforts will be in vain unless we rely upon the Holy Spirit. This cannot just be a theological idea, but the reality which we experience. Proclamation made "in the power of the Holy Spirit" will evoke conversion. Otherwise it may be tickling the ears of our listeners, and satisfying the intellect, but with no intrinsic power to arouse a response of repentance and faith. When Peter stood up at Pentecost to speak to his contemporaries, everything had changed. He was now speaking with the fire of the Holy Spirit. His proclamation was anointed with power from on high. He had no fear, since the Holy Spirit gives a boldness to speak and provides the words to speak. His words were the words of God and they pierced the hearts of his listeners, who were called to conversion. One of the African bishops at the Synod on evangelisation, somewhat tongue in cheek, made the telling observation, "When Peter gave one sermon at Pentecost, 3,000 were converted; we give 3,000 sermons and nobody is converted!" What is the difference? The power of the Holy Spirit!

Jesus had promised the apostles, "You will receive power when the Holy Spirit comes upon you and then you will be my witnesses" (Acts 1:8). We cannot proclaim Jesus effectively by our own efforts, insights or learning. The apostles did not proclaim Christ "in doctrine" but "in the power of the Holy Spirit". There is a difference. The apostles are described as "those who preached to you the good news through the Holy Spirit" (1 Pet 1:12). Peter says, "Whoever preaches let it be 'with the words of God'" (1 Pet 4:11). This is not a doctrinal presentation or a moral exhortation. It is charismatic preaching in the fire of the Spirit. Jesus warned them that they would be called to give witness before unbelievers, "But when they hand you over do not worry about how to speak or what to say; what you are to say will be given to you when the time comes; because it is not you who will be speaking; the Spirit of your Father will be speaking in you" (Mt 10:19).

Fan Into a Flame the Gift

Pope John Paul II at the beginning of the millennium wrote to the whole Church,

> Over the years, I have often repeated the summons to the new evangelisation. I do so again now, especially in order to insist that we must rekindle in ourselves the impetus of the beginnings and allow ourselves to be filled with the ardour of the apostolic preaching which followed Pentecost.[21]

This is a call "to fan into a flame" the gift that God gave us when hands were laid upon us in Confirmation (cf 2Tim 1:6). Each one needs the experience of a new Pentecost. Pope John XXIII prayed at the opening of the Second Vatican Council, "Lord, renew in our days your wonders as by a new Pentecost."[22] This prayer has been answered in a marvellous way by the Lord. Many within the Church are experiencing this grace of a new outpouring of the Holy Spirit upon us. This is happening in many streams of renewal, but not the least through the burgeoning Charismatic Renewal which is now estimated to have touched the lives of 200 million Catholics around the globe.

The Spirit is being poured out in an unprecedented way because these are desperate times for the Church and the world. The Church suffers from a crisis of faith within its members. So often "good Catholics" are persuaded by the voices of the secular elite of Western society who have largely abandoned the ways of God for an ideology driven by what pleases the individual. There is no accountability to God or to the richness of Christian heritage. In this crisis the Holy Spirit has sovereignly intervened. As people open up to this experience of the new Pentecost they find again clarity of faith, the fire of a new love for God, and the courage to preach the gospel in these troubled times.

On the eve of Pentecost 1998 Pope John Paul II, addressing hundreds of thousands of people from the various new movements and communities gathered in St Peter's Square, made a dramatic appeal, "Open yourselves docilely to the gifts of the Spirit! Accept gratefully the charisms which the Spirit never ceases to bestow on us".[23] He went on to assert strongly that the Church is essentially both institutional and charismatic; it would be erroneous to opt for one dimension over the other.

A Culture of Pentecost

The Popes have called for a "culture of Pentecost" which will sustain the "new evangelisation".[24] Addressing the Charismatic Renewal Pope John Paul II said: "In our time that is so hungry for hope, make the Holy Spirit known and loved. Help bring to life that 'culture of Pentecost' that alone can make fruitful the civilisation of love... never tire of praying 'Come Holy Spirit! Come! Come!'".[25] In a culture of Pentecost we are more deeply aware of the activity of the Holy Spirit in our life and mission, and we are more expectant of the movement of the Spirit leading, guiding and directing our evangelising activity. Within a culture of Pentecost we are open to the transforming work of the Holy Spirit, changing us from within so we become authentic witnesses of the love of God. We let the Holy Spirit give us the wisdom to know when and how to move, when to speak and when not to speak. We are open to the Holy Spirit giving the words to speak and the way to proclaim.

In a culture of Pentecost the Holy Spirit will give the authority and conviction to speak, and will convince the listener by witnessing interiorly to the truth of what is proclaimed. The Holy Spirit will bring consolation to those who need healing. The Spirit will comfort the afflicted but will also afflict the comfortable by convicting them of sin. The Holy Spirit comes as a burning fire igniting the heart with love for God and others, but also purifying the soul like gold in a furnace. A new infusion of the Holy Spirit brings new life, recreation as sons and daughters of God. The Holy Spirit unites us in a communion of love and equips us to become evangelists. A community of missionary disciples needs to be cultivating this culture of Pentecost at all times.

A Current of Grace for the Church

The Holy Spirit is the soul of the Church. Each member of the Church needs to experience in adult life a personal Pentecost, a releasing of the power of one's baptism and confirmation so that we can be genuine witnesses in our contemporary world. This "big grace" is called "baptism in the Holy Spirit". The term is taken from the New Testament and refers to an *immersion* in the Spirit. The experience of this new Pentecost is intrinsically connected to sacramental Baptism. In our adult life, when we open to this grace what was given in our sacramental Baptism becomes actualised more fully. By our adult "yes" to what was given in the sacrament we allow the fruit of our Baptism to be manifest.

Pope Francis calls the Charismatic Renewal a "current of grace in the Church and for the Church". Speaking to a large gathering of the Charismatic Renewal in Rome he said, "I expect from you that you share with all, in the Church, the grace of baptism in the Holy Spirit"[26]. He is convinced of its necessity for the Church's mission in today's world. The Pope is clear that the Renewal is not a movement in the common sociological sense. It does not have a founder. Rather it erupted in the Church as a sovereign work of the Spirit.

While not all Catholics are intended to be card-carrying members of the Renewal no Catholic can dismiss the urgency of opening more to the grace of a new pentecost. Again in 2015 speaking to a rally of the Renewal the Pope urged everyone present "to share with all in the Church the baptism in the Spirit you have received. You have lived this experience; share it in the Church. And this is the most important service that can be given to everyone in the Church."[27] Pope Francis gives his reason for saying this – the baptism in the Spirit brings a personal encounter with Jesus Christ, who changes us, and empowers us to bring this good news to others. In 2015 during a priests' charismatic retreat in the Basilica of John Lateran attended by over a thousand priests from all over the world Pope Francis instructed his brother priests to bring the experience of the baptism in the Spirit to all their parishioners "so that the Holy Spirit could bring about that personal encounter with Jesus Christ, which changes lives."[28]

The Journey of Pope Francis

Pope Francis has more than once admitted that originally in Buenos Aires as a young priest he had angrily dismissed the Charismatic Renewal since he judged they "confuse the Holy Spirit with a Samba school". He had also criticised charismatics for "claiming to be in possession of the Holy Spirit".[29] Things changed when as Cardinal of Buenos Aires he began to give talks to the annual charismatic school of formation. He challenged the lay people to share the joy of the gospel and not to be focussed on themselves but to go out to the peripheries to bring the good news to the poor. He was drawn by the authentic quality of the worship, and began to turn up at ecumenical charismatic conferences, just to be present and to listen.

In June 2006 Cardinal Bergoglio arranged for a major ecumenical event to be held in the seven-thousand seat capacity Luna Park stadium.[30] Fr Raniero Cantalamessa, the Capuchin preacher to the papal household, and a number of Pentecostal pastors were present. More Catholics than evangelicals crammed into the arena. When the Cardinal was invited to speak he came to the stage and fell to his knees asking for the preachers to pray over him. They gathered around him and prayed for more of the Holy Spirit upon him. This was the turning point. Many would say that his preaching from that time onwards had greater fervour, passion, urgency and clarity. He became more directly a promoter of the Renewal. Just a few months before taking part in the conclave he had been appointed by the Episcopal conference as spiritual director for the Renewal in Argentina. Now as Pope he actively encourages and challenges the world-wide Renewal.

To be Baptised in the Spirit

John the Baptist said, "I baptise with water, but the one who comes after me I am not fit to undo his sandal straps. He will baptise you with fire and the Holy Spirit" (Lk 3:16, cf Jn 1:32-33). Jesus is the one who baptises with the Holy Spirit. "To baptise" has a metaphoric significance here: It means "to immerse, to flood, to bathe completely and to submerge", just like we experience when we jump bodily into a pool of water. Jesus "gives the Holy Spirit without measure" (Jn 3:34). The biblical phrase refers more to Pentecost than to the sacrament of baptism. We see this clearly when Jesus, referring to Pentecost, promises, "John baptised with water, but not many days from now you will be baptised in the Holy Spirit" (Acts 1:5).

Just as Jesus experienced the anointing of the Spirit come upon him in the Jordan River, so after he returned to the Father he fulfilled his promise to share this anointing with us. What he experienced in his humanity in the Jordan, we experience through the outpouring of the Holy Spirit as a new Pentecost. The resurrected Jesus continues the essential work of "baptising in the Spirit". This new outpouring of the Spirit which the Lord has chosen to bring to his Church in these days is meant for all God's people. It is not an exclusive or elitist experience for a select few. Nor is it the same as a spiritual retreat or the taking of vows which are in themselves new experiences of grace for holiness and evangelisation. It is more fundamental to the Christian life; a desperately needed in-filling of the Holy Spirit, and is experienced as an extraordinary power given from on high. How can we possibly explain why this has happened? The reason is ultimately hidden in the mysterious will of God. It has pleased the Lord to renew his Church in these times by this means. That's all we can say; but with great gratitude for this immense gift for our age.

Related to Sacramental Baptism

As Catholics it is important to understand how this experience of "baptism in the Spirit" is integrated with the sacrament of Baptism. We say that this outpouring of the Spirit actualises and revives our Baptism. The sacrament received in infancy comes alive. When Baptism is validly administered to children it is guaranteed to be efficacious. However, its power needs to be released by our own personal decision as we grow into adulthood. The effect of any sacrament depends on divine grace but this divine grace is not fully fruitful without our "yes" to God's action.

In Catholic theology we make a distinction between everything that depends on God's grace in the sacrament, the work already accomplished,[31] and everything that depends on our free consent and fervent disposition, the work yet to be accomplished through our deeper "yes". So when baptised as a child we are united with Christ, adopted as sons and daughters of God, and brought into the people of God. This truly happens. This is the work accomplished. The grace and the seal of Baptism have been given. Yet the full power of the sacrament remains "unreleased" without our personal response of faith. As Scripture says, "The one who believes and is baptised shall be saved" (Mk 16:16). Baptism is a sign of faith, but when we are baptised as a child, the faith provided is that of the parents and the community gathered. It remains incomplete until we, as adults, are able to wholeheartedly profess our faith in Jesus as our Saviour and Lord, and ask for the Holy Spirit to become more active within us and through us.

Of course the act of faith is only possible by the grace of God, but it requires our cooperation, our free will to say "yes" to what God is doing. So Baptism and faith go together and cannot be separated. As St Basil wrote, "Truly, faith and baptism, these two modes of salvation, are bound indivisibly to one another, because if faith receives its perfection from baptism, baptism is founded on faith."[32] This is clear from the early Church's practice of preparing candidates for Baptism as adults, and our recapturing of this in the current RCIA program. Baptism presumes faith and then Baptism is the "seal of faith". Paul says to the Ephesians, "When you had heard the word of truth, the gospel of your salvation, and had believed in him, (you) were marked with the seal of the promised Holy Spirit" (Eph 1:13) Here the "seal" refers to Baptism, which was preceded by hearing the word and believing.

A Second Conversion

For those who have been baptised as a child this new outpouring of the Spirit is a renewal of Baptism and often a "second conversion" experience. The graces of Baptism become more manifest in a person's life for growth in holiness. This is also the case with the sacrament of Confirmation which develops, confirms and fulfils the work of Baptism. Indeed the renewal of Confirmation is particularly important for the work of evangelisation. This sacrament involves the laying on of hands by the bishop for the Holy Spirit to empower the candidate for mission. Through this sacrament the candidate receives "power from on high" to participate fully in the missionary work of the Church.

If Baptism is primarily an immersion into the Easter mystery of the saving death and resurrection of Jesus, Confirmation is primarily an immersion into the mystery of Pentecost! But when given at an early age the full appreciation of this reality cannot be appropriated. So when adults are prepared to receive a new outpouring of the Holy Spirit and make a personal "yes" for this to happen, the graces of Confirmation are released more fully. Under the grace of this "new Pentecost", people experience a new fire to evangelise rising in the heart, a new boldness to proclaim the word, and a new expectancy for signs and wonders to accompany the proclamation, and a new thirst for the salvation of all men and women.

This new outpouring of the Spirit, which we call "baptism in the Spirit" is a "big grace" from God, a gratuitous gift which cannot be induced. However, we can prepare ourselves to receive the gift, and we can ask for the gift. Jesus encourages us to ask for the Holy Spirit and to trust the gift will be given (Lk 11:9-13). Seraphim of Sarov said "the whole Christian life is simply one prolonged invocation of the Holy Spirit". Preparation for adults involves hearing the word of God preached, especially the basic kerygmatic proclamation, responding with genuine repentance, making a new "yes" to the saving love of Christ and surrendering one's life to the new in-filling of the Holy Spirit. Usually others will pray by laying on of hands being a witness to what Jesus will do. Jesus is the one who "baptises in the Spirit". The best environment for this to happen is in a loving community of brothers and sisters who are supporting the person in prayer and encouraging them to be open to all that the Lord would want to do.

"I Want that Joy"

Gerry was the youngest of six children in a Catholic family. A victim of domestic violence at home and being bullied at school, he suffered from deep-seated anxiety and raging anger. To vent his angry feelings and to suppress his emotional distress during high school years he took on boxing and martial arts. While this helped him win friends it also led him into a life-style of drinking, drugs and wild parties. A particularly virulent drug overdose frightened him and he dropped that scene and turned to the materialistic dream of making lots of money as the answer to life. This also left him empty. Retiring to the family farm he was sucked into a dark depression, contemplating suicide. He was now a young man with nowhere to go, and nothing to live for.

His sister invited him to a week-long evangelising retreat for young adults held in a large boarding school during the summer. He said that when he walked into the lobby of the school he was overwhelmed by the warmth of the welcome and the way "everyone was beaming". He felt intimidated by such joy, but deep in his heart he knew this is what he wanted. Yet he rushed to his room to put the earphones on to suppress this new stirring within him. At the opening Mass, in which two hundred young people were clapping, singing and praising God, he stood stolidly with his hands by his side and a stern face. But inside he was screaming, "Where are you God?" He says "I was angry with

God". He felt like God had overlooked him. He told God, "I want that joy! I would rather die than live without that joy!" He did not feel life was worth living if he continued to be burdened by fear and anger. He challenged God, "If this joy is real, show me this week".

He struggled through the first couple of days. But on the Reconciliation night he poured out the darkness of his sins to a priest in Confession. The priest told him, "Go and sit in front of the exposed Blessed Sacrament. As you are there with Jesus think about what type of man you want to be. Pour your heart out to God". Gerry did as he was told, crying out to the Lord for all he wanted from his life. He said the two strongest desires which arose in him were, "I want that joy!" and "I want to be a missionary!" A couple of nights later, when he was being prayed over by others, Gerry experienced being baptised in the Spirit. He said, "I felt the joy. I was over the moon. I felt I could run a mile and not lose pace. Nothing else mattered. I wanted to be nowhere else but here, with Jesus". A week later Gerry signed up for a year of ministry with a team which brings the gospel message to young people in Catholic schools. But as he was flying to Perth to begin the mission he all of a sudden felt totally unqualified to speak about God to others. But the Lord spoke to him, "Don't worry, now I have you back, I will give you the tools". During that year of ministry his testimony touched thousands of young people. Gerry now continues to live a committed Catholic life within a strong faith community and he loves to share his story of deliverance from darkness and his discovery of lasting joy.

A Big Grace for the New Evangelisation

In speaking about this grace of the "baptism in the Spirit" I am not claiming that the experience common to the Charismatic Renewal is the only way Catholics can be renewed in their Baptism. In fact, almost all of the new movements in the Church today have at their centre the desire to help others discover their full identity as baptised Catholics, and to consequently share in the grace of the "new evangelisation". However, I am unapologetically offering to all Catholics the opportunity to seek this "big grace", firstly because of its profound effect in my own life and the lives of countless others, but also because Pope Francis has asked us to let the whole Church know about this new, liberating "current of grace" in the Church today.

I am thoroughly convinced that the Holy Spirit is being poured out in our time primarily for the sake of the proclamation of the gospel. We need the ardour and faith conviction of the early Church if we are to be effective in our missionary efforts. And that fire and conviction is given by the Holy Spirit. We are to rekindle the gift that God gave us when hands were laid upon us by the successor of the apostles at Confirmation "for God did not give us a spirit of fear, but rather a spirit of power and of love and of self-control" (2 Tim 1:6-7).

An Ecumenical Grace

On the eve of Pentecost 2017 Pope Francis addressed a rally of 50,000 people at the Circus Maximus in Rome celebrating the golden jubilee of Catholic Charismatic Renewal. Affirming once again that this "current of grace" is for the whole Church, the Pope underlined that it is not just a grace for Catholics but an "ecumenical grace". It is a creative action of the Holy Spirit providing a new opportunity for unity. Drawing upon his experience of unity with Evangelicals and Pentecostals in Buenos Aires, the Pope emphasised that under the influence of the Holy Spirit our common confession that "Jesus is Lord" makes spiritual communion possible. We should not ignore or deny the doctrinal differences, but at the same time move together under this one confession of faith in the spirit of "reconciled diversity". By this term he means, that while there are diverse expressions of the Christian faith, we can walk together on this pilgrim journey with a spirit of unity forged through forgiveness and reconciliation.

The Pope is keen to have us reflect on the "hierarchy of truths" and to realise that the fundamental truths of the *kerygma* are shared by all. This is what unites us. Consequently, with so many Christian martyrs dying with the name of Jesus on their lips we can speak of an "ecumenism of blood". He says, "Those who are about to kill Christians do not ask, 'Are you Orthodox? Are you Catholic? Are you Evangelical? Are you Lutheran? Are you Calvinist?' No. They ask, 'Are you Christian?' If the answer is 'Yes' then your throat is cut, immediately."[33] We are united by the witness of the martyrs who shed their blood for Christ.

The Pope calls us to be committed to unity in order to bring the good news of Jesus to the immense number of people who do not know him. This unity "can no longer be a matter of mere diplomacy or forced compliance, but rather an indispensable path to evangelisation".[34] He is well aware that the greatest scandal, a real stumbling block to the unbeliever, is the division between Christians. We should not offer an image of a people divided and separated by quarrels, but a people united and mature in faith. The unbeliever needs to be able to say, "See how these Christians love one another". Our divisions impede the work of Christ. They give rise to criticisms, complaints and ridicule. Hence the urgency for a united evangelising effort.

Learning From One Another

Pope Francis is encouraging us not only to dialogue about the differences with mutual respect. He wants us to make friends with one another and work together to bring others to Christ. He encourages us to let go of a superior outlook. While in reality the fullness of truth is found in the Catholic Church, we must humbly admit that we can learn much from our brothers and sisters in other ecclesial communions. This receptive ecumenism means that our dialogue, as Pope John Paul II taught us, is not just an exchange of ideas but also an exchange of gifts.[35] The creativity of the Holy Spirit is such that we can actually learn from one another. Pope Francis says, "It is not just about being better informed about others, but rather about reaping what the Spirit has sown in them, which is also meant to be a gift to us".[36] The other ecclesial communions are not sparring partners, nor ecclesiological curiosities. They contain gifts from the Holy Spirit for us. With this insight the Popes are opening up for us a new pathway for ecumenism! Humbly, we Catholics ought not only ask how we differ from others, but also ask what we can learn from them.

Pope Francis is not naïve about the challenges involved in working together ecumenically. For a Catholic, to share about Jesus is also to offer fullness of communion within the Body of Christ, his Church. We do not only evangelise towards a conversion to personal relationship with Jesus, but we also want to see people initiated into the full sacramental life of the Church. When planning conferences or rallies with an ecumenical dimension we need to be open about our ecclesial vision, even though many Evangelical and Pentecostal groups do not share the same concerns. We would consider our evangelising work incomplete if people do not come into sacramental communion. Others may be content as long as people who have had some initial conversion find some sort of Christian fellowship. We, on the other hand, want to offer people the fullness of the gift that we possess, which includes Eucharistic communion. When evangelising together, these tensions can be present and need to be dialogued freely and honestly, and appropriate pastoral agreements made. However, rather than emphasise what we cannot do together it is always best to find ways for what we can do.

4
CHARISMATIC GIFTS

With the new outpouring of the Holy Spirit in our day we are experiencing the proliferation of charisms in a wonderful way. They give power to the new evangelisation. Pope John Paul II celebrated this new abundance of charisms:

> Whenever the Spirit intervenes, he leaves people astonished. He brings about events of amazing newness; he radically changes persons and history. This was the unforgettable experience of the Second Vatican Ecumenical Council during which, under the guidance of the same Spirit, the Church rediscovered the charismatic dimension of her constitutive elements.[37]

Within this new "current of grace", the Charismatic Renewal, which happened only a couple of years after the Council, charisms became more "normal" in the ordinary life of the Church. Previously, healings, prophecy and miracles, the so-called extraordinary manifestations, were only expected amongst saints and mystics. Now we are experiencing something of what it was like in the early Church, where the charisms were widely spread amongst the faithful and were often exercised for the proclamation of the good news.

Vatican II Declaration

Thankfully, Vatican II had already given the necessary theological foundation. After a debate on the Council floor about whether charisms were still intended for the Church, the bishops gave a resounding "yes". They stated clearly that the activity of the Holy Spirit is not only through the sacraments and ministries of the Church, but also through charisms:

> It is not only through the sacraments and the ministries of the Church that the Holy Spirit makes holy the People, leads them and enriches them with his virtues. Allotting his gifts according as he wills (cf. 1Cor 12:11), he also distributes special graces among the faithful of every rank. By these gifts he makes them fit and ready to undertake various tasks and offices for the renewal and building up of the Church, as it is written, "the manifestation of the Spirit is given to everyone for profit" (1Cor 12:7). Whether these charisms be very remarkable or more simple and widely diffused, they are to be received with thanksgiving and consolation since they are fitting and useful for the needs of the Church.[38]

St Paul gives several lists of charisms, none of which is intended to be exhaustive. In 1Corinthians 12 he catalogues some of the more prominent gifts – words of wisdom, words of knowledge, prophecy, faith, healing, miracles, discernment, tongues and interpretation of tongues. In Romans 12:6-8 Paul mentions prophecy, but also the more ordinary gifts of service, teaching, exhortation, giving, leading, and acts of mercy. In Ephesians 4:11-13 he lists gifts of apostles, prophets, evangelists, and pastors. Paul also refers to the vocational charisms of celibacy and marriage. Also we find in 1Peter 4:10-11 encouragement for the charisms of preaching and serving. In our contemporary experience we would add other charisms, such as hospitality, compassion, listening, administration, leadership, worship (music), intercession, voluntary poverty, creative arts, and many others.[39]

Features of Charisms

Charisms are to be distinguished from talents, which are natural abilities. Charisms are supernatural gifts flowing from the grace of our Baptism. They either enable what would otherwise be impossible or they elevate a natural endowment, such as music or hospitality, to a supernatural level. Charisms are given freely. It is not due to merit, nor something acquired through effort. Charisms are given for the sake of others. They are not for personal sanctification as such but for the upbuilding of the body of Christ, and to assist with the Church's evangelising activity.

The Church is both institutional and charismatic. Pope John Paul II taught that both of these dimensions are co-essential for the Church. "Without hierarchical authority the Church would be chaotic; without the charisms it would be dead."[40] The presence of charisms is not an optional extra in the fully functioning Church, but absolutely essential for its health. But it is good to distinguish between the sanctifying action of the Holy Spirit and the charismatic activity. The sacraments convey sanctifying grace; if we are open they make us holy. The seven interior gifts of the Spirit received at Confirmation are likewise the sanctifying work of the Spirit, making us holy and supporting the growth of virtue. In contrast the charismatic activity of the Holy Spirit is not about making us holy. The charisms are given for the building up the body of Christ and for strengthening the Church's missionary work.

Because the charisms are essential for the Church they need to be welcomed and supported. Rather than wait for them to manifest we ought to be actively cultivating them. Hilary of Poitiers (310-368), after listing the charisms given in 1Corinthians 12, exclaims, "Let us make use of such generous gifts!"[41] In another place he says,

> We who have been reborn through the sacrament of bap-

tism experience intense joy when we feel within us the first stirrings of the Holy Spirit. We begin to have insight into the mysteries of the faith; we are able to prophesy and speak with wisdom. We become steadfast in hope and receive abundant gifts of healing...These gifts enter us as a gentle rain. Little by little they bear abundant fruit.[42]

Cyril of Jerusalem likewise urges those preparing for Baptism, "Prepare your souls for the reception of the heavenly charisms," and prays, "God grant that you may be worthy of the charism of prophecy".[43]

Word Gifts

It is noteworthy that the gift of prophecy was highly prized in the early Church. Prophecy is when someone speaks in God's name, communicating a message that is not one's own but comes from God.[44] Paul frequently exhorts his communities to ask for prophecy. He wants them to earnestly desire prophecy and never to despise it (1Cor 14: 4-5, 39; Thess 5:20). When he lists who is important in the Church he mentions apostles first and then prophets (1Cor 12:28). Prophets often brought guidance to the community (Acts 13:2). Contrary to the popular notion that prophets foretell the future, in fact they more than often speak God's word for the community *right now*. The word they speak is encouraging, strengthening, and in tune with God's heart for the people at this moment. Sometimes it is a challenging word calling to repentance but always it builds up the community.

The word gifts are particularly useful in the new evangelisation. During preaching or teaching the gift of knowledge brings a sharpness of insight into the meaning of a scriptural text or a particular truth of the faith. The gift of wisdom can help the one proclaiming to sense what God is doing at that time and to act accordingly when calling for a response. The gift of prophecy can be used when praying with particular people. The Lord provides a word that is specifically for this person and can be a great source of encouragement and enlightenment for them. The gift of word of knowledge also can identify hidden areas which God wants to heal and help the person to claim that healing.

Pastoral Care

Cultivating an expectation of charisms is always risky since they can easily be abused. The answer is not in suppressing the gifts, but in giving good teaching and solid pastoral care. As Paul says, "Do not quench the Spirit. Do not despise the words of the prophets, but test everything" (1Thes 5:20-21). Testing, or discernment, is necessary. For example, in the case of prophecy the pastoral leaders would need to look at the life of the prophet and see whether it is bearing good fruit, showing signs of genuine humility, love and obedience. They would also look at the words spoken and see that they are in conformity with Scripture and the teaching of the Church, and look at the tone of the word and its impact upon the people, whether it impacts positively or negatively.

In general, good discernment of charisms should seek the following characteristics in their exercise:[45] the charism focuses attention on Jesus Christ and gives glory to him, rather than drawing attention to the individual; the charism is exercised in full accord with the teachings of the Church; the charism is in harmony with what the Holy Spirit is already doing in the present context (however, the community should also be open to a surprise of the Spirit); the charism contributes to the building up of the body of Christ in love; the person exercising the charism has a spirit of obedience to Church authority; the charism is exercised simply and humbly as a free gift in the Spirit.

The ultimate criterion is practical love. As Paul says, "Strive for the greater gifts. And I will show you a still more excellent way" (1Cor 12:31). He then goes on to pronounce that he could have the gift of tongues, prophecy, knowledge, faith, poverty, or martyrdom, but if he is without love they will count for nothing. He is not saying love is a charism. Rather all the charisms are only authentic if they are exercised with love. Love for others is the only way charisms can be exercised with real benefit for the Church.

Charisms in the History of the Church

In the early Church the supernatural gifts, or charisms, were expected to be received when adults were baptised. St Cyprian of Carthage (200-258AD) includes the power to heal the sick and cast out demons amongst the supernatural gifts bestowed at Baptism.[46] St Hilary of Poitiers (300-368AD) likewise speaks of the charism of healing given at Baptism.[47] These and other witnesses believed firmly that at Baptism many charisms were given that would in time become manifest in the believers lives as they matured more in their way of discipleship.

St Irenaeus (115-202AD) testifies to "many brothers in the Church who have the prophetic charisms, who speak in many tongues, who reveal the secrets of men's hearts to their benefit, and who explain the mysteries of God".[48] He speaks of supernatural activity done by believers, bringing many to conversion:

> Those who are in truth his disciples, receiving grace from him, perform miracles in his name so as to promote the welfare of others, according to the gift which each one has received from him. For some do certainly and truly drive out devils......Others have foreknowledge of things to come: they see visions and utter prophecies. Still others heal the sick by laying their hands upon them, and they are made

whole. Yes, moreover, the dead have even been raised up and remained among us for many years.[49]

The Decline of Charisms

However, in the fourth century the use of charisms began to decline. A major factor in this decline was the heresy of Montanism, which put an exaggerated emphasis on the gift of prophecy in particular, but other charisms as well. What started as an enthusiastic prophetic movement ended in heresy. The Montanists began to believe that they alone had God's word for the Church and people would do better listening to their prophecies than to the word of the bishops. This extremist and deviant use of charisms put a shock wave into the Church, especially when a reputable figure such as Tertullian embraced this highly controversial prophetic movement and sought to defend their doctrines. Church leaders began to shy away from charismatic activity as potentially dangerous and divisive.

Because of abuses the pastors of the Church began to exercise their authority more strongly and gradually the use of charisms amongst the laity became more sporadic and eventually disappeared. The charisms were seen to be associated with the ordained clergy, not the laity. There was also a growing tendency to identify the use of charisms with personal holiness. The "clericalisation" of the charisms was aided by the presumption that priests, monks and religious were the really holy ones. But while charisms disappeared amongst the majority of Christ's faithful, they were still expected especially in saintly figures, and indeed became an accepted sign of sainthood. Church history is full of charismatic preachers, evangelists, prophets and teachers. Many of the saints had extraordinary gifts of healing, miracles, deliverance from demons, discernment of spirits, words of knowledge, and supernatural wisdom.

When we take a broad sweep of history we can also see waves of charismatic awakenings, during which the Spirit was poured out in new and dynamic ways. The charisms were not lost entirely to the life of the Church, but lost to its public life and relegated to a relatively insignificant place in theology. In practice they were no longer seen as essential to the life of the Church. In the light of this history it is somewhat humbling for us to realise that the reawakening of the charisms in a widespread way in the twentieth century was initiated by spiritual movements outside of the perimeter of the Catholic Church. This fact alone should make us grateful for this ecumenical grace brought by the Holy Spirit who is not confined to any boundaries.

A Life of Holiness

While the use of supernatural gifts is in no way a sign of holiness, we still need to be working on a holy way of life to be able to exercise these gifts responsibly. Charismatic gifts do not prove one is holy. But they will not be sustained in good order except by growth in holiness. If we want to evangelise in the power of the Spirit it is crucial that we have our own personal journey of intimacy with Jesus. It means spending long hours with him before the Blessed Sacrament, adoring him as the love of your life. It means reading the scriptures prayerfully and meditating on the word often. It means growing in humility. The stronger the current of electricity flowing through a conductor, the more insulation needed. Otherwise it is wasted. The same for the Spirit-filled Christian. The more you are used by the Lord with the charism of healing or prophecy or miracles, the more humble you will need to be. Humility is your "insulation" from disaster. Also, and most importantly, I need to repeat, that whenever we are exercising the gifts we must do so with practical love. Paul tells us this is the higher way and the only way the gifts of the Spirit can be exercised without causing damage within the body of Christ. Included in this is a genuine heart of compassion for those to whom you minister, and a sensitivity to their deepest needs.

Signs and Wonders Today

When preaching occurs in the power of the Holy Spirit things happen. We are told that when Jesus spoke people were astonished. They said to one another, "Here is a teaching that is new and with authority behind it; he gives orders to unclean spirits and they obey him" (Mk 1:27). When Jesus sent his apostles out he instructed them, "As you go, proclaim the kingdom of heaven is close at hand. Cure the sick, raise the dead, cleanse the lepers, cast out devils" (Mt 10:7-8). He clearly expected something to happen when they proclaimed the word. As with Jesus, so with his Church, when we move under the anointing of the Spirit. In the power of the Spirit "signs and wonders" occur as an exterior witness of the truth of the word proclaimed. Paul reminded the Corinthians, "in my speeches and sermons I gave, there were none of the arguments that belong to philosophy; only a demonstration of the power of the Holy Spirit" (1Cor 2:4). When Philip preached the good news in Samaria we are told the people welcomed the message "because they had heard of the miracles he worked or because they saw them for themselves" (Act 8:6). The good news was visible in the signs that accompanied its proclamation (Mk 16:20).

Damian Stayne, a Catholic layman, who has a ministry of healing and deliverance based in Surrey England, testifies to one prayer service for healing when through a word of knowledge and prayer 51 people experienced their tumours either shrink or disappear altogether. He maintains the healing ministry is not just for experts but for all believers. Just as in the early Church, he says, we need to believe there is no sickness that Christians cannot heal. He tells the story of a team of lay street evangelisers in London, who were moving about in the CBD seeking words from the Lord about who they should approach. They felt drawn by the Spirit to talk to a man in a wheel-chair outside of a busy station. They asked him politely, "Would you like us to pray for you?" He replied, "I am not a Christian". They replied, "It doesn't matter". So the man said "Oh well, it can't do any harm". So as they began to pray the man began to shake and scream; a demon was manifesting. This caused quite a deal of consternation among bystanders. Someone called the police, thinking that the man was being harassed by strangers. But by the time the police arrived the man had been delivered and had given his life to Jesus. He stood up and pushed the chair to the pavement, not needing it anymore. The officer rushed in demanding, "What's happening here?" The man said, "I am healed! I don't need my chair anymore!" The man joined the team and continued with them letting others know what had happened to him. Under the anointing of the new evangelisation we can expect signs and wonders as the Holy Spirit witnesses to the unbeliever.

5
CHALLENGES WE FACE

Preaching the gospel in a post-Christian society has countless challenges. Our situation today is similar to that of the first Christians who boldly confronted the pagan Roman Empire with the good news of Jesus. As with them, our hope is in the Lord, and he has promised he will be with us (Mt 28:20). The prevailing culture is largely indifferent towards religion in general, but in recent years there has been increasing hostility towards Christianity and all it represents. The modern secularised mind-set has no place for God, and is shut out from supernatural reality. Yet, not so surprisingly, people still show an interest in "the supernatural", using Ouiji boards, séances, crystal balls, palm reading, tarot cards, mediums and a whole range of New Age devices. Religion is far from being killed off, no matter how much the neo-atheists would want to see it disappear. This inquisitiveness about supernatural phenomena and quest for some sort of spiritual experience creates a favourable climate for the proclamation of the gospel, especially when it is accompanied by healing ministry.

A New Ideology
The main protagonists of Western culture have abandoned Christianity and have opted for a new ideology of secularism and radical individualism. As Pope John Paul II used to say, "to lose God means to lose our humanity". We can no longer rely upon the culture to support our ideals and aspirations about what it means to be a hu-

man being. Alasdair MacIntyre argues that in this culture people are governed not so much by faith or reason, but by emotivism: the idea that all moral choices are nothing more than expressions of what the choosing individual feels is right.[50] To live "after virtue" is to be in a society which is "a collection of strangers, each pursuing his or her own interests under minimal constraints".[51] There are no objective standards, no religious or cultural traditions that are binding, no social obligations, unless personally chosen. Everyone is to follow his or her own desires, no matter what the society, or the Church or any other moral or religious authority says. Rod Dreher comments, "Here is the end point to modernity: the autonomous freely choosing individual, finding meaning in no one but himself".[52] Individuals think they have the right to define their own concept of existence, their own meaning for existence, and their own understanding of what is important for human life, no matter how bizarre it may be.

Decision for Christ and Community

What does it mean to preach the gospel in this desert-like cultural context which is inimical to the message? It means firstly we must focus upon leading people to a personal encounter with Jesus as their Saviour, and to submit to him as Lord. We cannot rely on the tight Catholic social grid of previous days. It has gone. Christian families understandably worry for their children growing up in this social environment which is erosive of Christian beliefs and values. All the more reason for intentionally creating the conditions whereby people feel free to make a personal choice in regard to their received faith. We cannot rely solely upon teaching of doctrine, instruction on the commandments and participation in liturgical celebrations. Too often people are catechised without being evangelised.

Our catechism needs to be always centred in the proclamation of the *kerygma*. In the next chapter we will speak more about what this means. Unless young people discover the experience of God's love and are won by the beauty of Jesus crucified and risen any amount of teaching of the faith will bear little fruit, and could in fact be counterproductive. Gone are the days when it makes sense to introduce young people to the sacraments without opening up for them the fundamental gospel message. Sacramental participation needs to be motivated by a desire to worship flowing from a living encounter with Christ and a growing relationship of love and gratitude for such a Saviour. Secondly, we must combat individualism by working hard to develop faith communities which can provide the support we need to hold firmly to our beliefs and values. I will deal with the crucial need for community in a later chapter.

A Christian Humanism

As Church we need to be aware of self-secularising ideas and practices. The mind-set of the culture within which we swim infiltrates our own minds. We become confused in our thinking. An example of this is the way some people in the Church speak in a well-intentioned way about the "autonomy of earthly affairs". They misinterpret *Gaudium et Spes*, the Vatican II document on the Church in the modern world. In this document the bishops were teaching that areas of enquiry such as psychology, sociology, natural science etc. have their own laws and these need to be respected as such. In that sense they are recognised as autonomous. But this was never intended to mean they were disconnected from God. In this secularist climate the tendency is to claim that the legitimately secular realm is separate from the supernatural and so is not really answerable to God. To the contrary, Pope John Paul II was adamant that Christ is the model of any authentic humanism. And Pope Benedict XVI said, "a humanism that excludes God is an inhuman humanism".

In the secularist mind-set people will readily misinterpret Jesus' injunction, "Render to Caesar what is Caesar's and to God what is God's" (Mt 22:21). Yes we pay taxes, live according to the law of the land, and respect lawful civil authority. In that way we render to Caesar what is Caesar's. But this does not mean an exclusion of God from the public sphere, as if God is only active in places of religious worship and religious institutions. When Jesus says "Render to God what is God's", that means everything! That means he is Lord of all! Jesus is the Alpha and the Omega, the beginning and end of all history. His death and resurrection is the pivotal moment of all history. Every nation, every world leader, every potentate is ultimately under his authority and answerable to him.

Proclaim Christ, Not Just the Fruits

Another subtle shift which is self-defeating in the face of our contemporary challenge is the tendency to celebrate the fruits of Christianity, but to leave Christ out of it.[53] So Catholic schools and hospitals fearful of offending people of other faiths will remove the crucifixes from the wall, and have multi-faith chapels. Christ is not to be mentioned for fear of offending Buddhists or Muslims. But it is fallacious to separate the ideas and values of Christ from Christ himself. In today's society much of the legacy of Christianity remains, especially in the protection of human rights. But as a Church we ring our own death knell if we seek to hold only to the fruits of Christianity and don't explicitly proclaim Christ. Our social welfare agencies operate on the principles of justice, love and mercy, and the dignity of each human person, but often this is without any reference to Christ who is the source of these principles and values. We are complicit in our own secularisation. The new evangelisation calls for a fearless proclamation of Christ at the centre of all that we do, and makes the witness of our works a more powerful light in the world.

Science and Technology

We live in a context where people genuinely believe that science and technology will save us. Or at least that technology will give us control over our destinies. Who could deny that we benefit immensely from technology? Advances are accelerating in their rapidity. Who can remember when we did not have computers and smart phones? Seems like the dark ages long ago. But are we sufficiently aware of how technology is changing us? It is an ideology that is reshaping how we perceive reality. In one sense technology is value neutral, like a garden spade that can be used to dig a garden or to hit someone over the head in rage. It is just an instrument. But, more deeply, technology as a world-view trains us to prefer what is new and innovative over what is old and familiar. We mindlessly move into the future, uncritically accepting what is the latest invention. The technological mind-set refuses any limits on its creativity and hence destroys tradition.[54] Here it can become dangerous to humanity. The technological devotee says, "If we can do it, we must be free to do it". In this mindset questions about why we should or should not do it don't make a lot of sense. For example, all the questions around the morality of *in vitro* fertilisation (IVF), the consequent necessity to freeze unwanted embryos, and the inevitable extermination of countless unborn lives, are irrelevant to the technological mind. A mentality of self-sufficient humanity, which has illusory control over our destiny, prevails.

The new evangelisation can burst this bubble, not so much by endless argumentation, but by a demonstration of the power of God's Holy Spirit. The scientific/technological mind has no room for the supernatural. The beauty of the baptism in the Holy Spirit is that it demonstrates the lie of this closed mentality. Pope John Paul II speaking to charismatic leaders said:

> At this moment in the Church's history, the Charismatic

Renewal can play a significant role in promoting the much needed defence of Christian life in societies where secularism and materialism have weakened many people's ability to respond to the Spirit and to discern God's call. Your contribution to the re-evangelisation of society will be made in the first place by personal witness to the indwelling Spirit.[55]

Earlier the Pope had shared with leaders of the Renewal that as a boy he complained to his father that he had trouble with his mathematics. His father gave him a prayer to the Holy Spirit and told him to pray that prayer every day. The Pope confided he had been faithful to that instruction from his father. He went on to say:

> The world is much in need of this action of the Holy Spirit….Materialism is the negation of the spiritual, and this is why we need the action of the Holy Spirit… the Holy Spirit comes to the human spirit, and from this moment we begin to live again, to find our very selves, to find our identity, our total humanity. Consequently, I am convinced that this movement is a very important component in the total renewal of the Church, in this spiritual renewal of the Church.[56]

Consumerist Society

Christianity within a consumerist society is in danger of succumbing to the tenets of the prevailing culture that worships the self and material comfort. In a narcissistic culture what matters is *my* personal agenda for *my* happiness, and *my* personal comfort regardless of others. What Paul calls "the flesh" dominates. We are driven to self-glorification, the impetus to be number one before others and enjoy their highest esteem. Otherwise we will feel diminished and insignificant. My self-worth is dependent on my achievements and what others think of me. The "flesh" is also operative in the thrust towards self-gratification. "I want it for me, now". Advertisers play on these base self-indulgent desires constantly, seeking to persuade people to want more and more so they will buy more and more. Rather than live on real needs, people are inspired by false needs to crave for what they do not really need at all. While the pursuit of consumer goods seems liberating, in fact it is a seductive form of captivity which destroys the soul.

The culture seeks comfort at all cost. The flip side of this is the avoidance of pain at all costs. The inner imperative is "I will not serve", unless of course there is a kick-back for me. In this sort of culture, where desire for selfish gain dominates, we believe we are entitled to a painless life of privilege and plenty, even if it is at the expense of others. Any talk of self-sacrifice is alien and unwanted. A final "flesh desire" fed by this culture is the refusal to be accountable to any authority or tradition, unless is suits me to do so. The imperative is "I will do it my way". We have already discussed something of this rugged individualism which will not answer to any community or social entity, apart from what is forced through civil law.

What drives the personal agenda in this modern culture is self and the need for "self-fulfilment". The language of the gospel is foreign and rejected. Any mention of losing one's life to find it, of dying to self for the sake of a greater 'yes' is unwelcome news. Hence the challenge to meet this generation dedicated to the "selfie" with the proclamation of the gospel. But all is far from lost. Recent research shows that many Australians across the board are open to receiving a spiritual message if it is delivered in an informal way and done with sensitivity.[57] Many are genuinely seeking for spiritual answers and are open to exploring options. Opportunities abound for fruitful conversations, especially at turning points or crises in life's journey when people are asking the deeper questions.

Joyful Witness

We know the answer to the deepest longing in the heart of every person is Jesus. If the quest is for self-fulfilment we can aid people to discover that the greatest joy is found in Jesus. People dedicated to self-indulgence are liable at some stage to slide into bewildering depression because the satisfaction they crave can never be found outside of God. Here is our entry point for the good news. However, to reach across the divide to people lost in the modern spiritual desert we need to be proclaiming the right message. Often our message is too negative and dark. We can appear to be obsessed with putting our finger into the wound caused by sin and laying condemnation on others, without even meaning to do so. We need to proclaim first that Jesus came to bring fullness of life.

If all we proclaim is "salvation from sin" the modern mind may not initially be open to receive the message. It can appear too negative and condemning, since it first points the finger at the sin. The Christian tradition has another way to come at the message. The new outpouring of the Spirit opens up the more positive dimension of the message – the new creation brought to us through the death and resurrection of Jesus. He is risen and he brings new life. We offer the joy of being reborn in Christ.

Friedrich Nietzsche, the father of modern atheism, looked around at the people of his time and observed they were a sad and gloomy lot. He is reputed to have said, "These Christians say they are redeemed; but they sure don't look like it". Maybe he was referring to a type of Christianity which is far removed from the gospel. The default mode of this style of Christianity is to be bemoaning our sins, feeling our unworthiness of salvation, possibly scraping home to heaven but only after many painful years in Purgatory. There is little joy! When they pray to the Father "thy will be done" they bow their heads in resignation, preparing for the worst! They act as if God is the enemy of pleasure and joy.

Whether we intended it or not, somehow the modern world has concluded that we Christians are against having a joyful life. I heard recently that a group of wealthy militant atheists funded an advertising campaign on London buses. The large caption read, "God probably doesn't exist. So stop worrying and enjoy life". What is the presumption here? That Christian faith takes the joy out of life! Better not to believe, and you will be happier, free of all the guilt and condemnation. It also says something about the way God is perceived in the popular mind – as an oppressive figure, rather than a liberating redeemer.

Now I don't mean that awareness of sin is not part of the gospel message. But it is not the first thing to be proclaimed! Otherwise the joyful character of the gospel can be obscured. There is something more to Amazing Grace than "saved a wretch like me". The new outpouring of the Spirit is a new "current of grace" for the Church. Pope Paul VI called it a "chance for the Church and the world". How is this so? Well partly because it allows us to respond to our salvation won for us as a new life in Jesus Christ. Rather than the gloomy pessimism of Nietzsche's time we proclaim a new vision of fullness of life in Christ, as he promised (Jn 10:10). We can celebrate the splendour of the new life God has brought to us. We are not left at the foot of the cross weeping for our sins, but we are also encountering the Risen Christ within whom we find fullness of life. Nietzsche once said, "I will only believe in a God who dances". He obviously had not read Zephaniah, "And the father will dance on the day of joy He will rejoice over you and renew you in his love" (Zeph 3:17). We go forth to proclaim the good news of God's saving love to our contemporaries with great joy in our hearts. This is contagious Christianity that not even the cynics of our time will ultimately be able to resist.

From Market Experts to Saints

Our evangelising can also become corrupted if we turn it into a crass marketing campaign, with strategic planning, motivational posters and performance indicators. God is not a commodity.[58] While we can learn from the marketing world about ways of communicating and how to attract people to come to events, we need to be careful that we don't become complicit with the consumerist mentality. We are not selling a commodity, but are inviting people into a personal encounter with Jesus, which happens by grace not by market forces or manipulative techniques. We can fall into the trap of imitating the strategies of corporate management. But the work of evangelisation is more personal. There is always an institutional dimension to evangelising but it is not qualifications and professional status that will make the work effective. Rather it will be personal holiness, wisdom, discernment, and prudential judgement. Cardinal Ratzinger made the comment:

> Saints, in fact reformed the Church in depth not by working up plans for new structures, but by reforming themselves. What the Church needs in order to respond to the needs of people in every age is holiness, not management.[59]

Church: Bearer of Absolute Truth

A major obstacle before the new evangelisation is the prevailing attitude that all religion is a human construct and all religions are on the same level. In our secular culture people resist any notion of a human community that is the bearer of a uniquely precious gift from God for all. It may be fine for you, they will say, but it's not for me. The idea that the Church could be the chosen instrument to bring the message of salvation to all men and women becomes particularly unacceptable, even obnoxious. This prevailing egalitarian individualistic attitude undermines many Christians in their confidence in having something important to give.⁶⁰ They are portrayed as arrogant, even if they offer the gift humbly, not as their own but as the gospel handed down faithfully from one generation to the next.

We know in faith that God has chosen a people as his own and has revealed himself to them, commissioning them to share his plan of salvation with all men and women. But many of our contemporaries will not have a bar of it. Not because they are necessarily bad people, but simply because they live in a cultural mind-set which has no room for a claim to absolute truth and no tolerance for anyone or any group who purport to have the true way to live. Religion can be tolerated in the society as long as it does not impinge upon this closed mind to God and the ways of God. Evangelising is offensive since it offers what has been revealed by God, and consequently proposes sure answers to many questions that otherwise would be difficult or impossible to answer.

Our secular culture rejects the notion that any human community enjoys a privileged relationship with God. This levelling mentality is a powerful undertow that can drag down Christians. They can tend to adopt the attitudes of those around them. As seductive as this mentality is, we must resist its allurement. It is rooted in the dismissal of God and his work in saving history. The Church is not only a human construct, but divinely founded and sustained. We are definitely a community of sinners, who cannot crow about our accomplishments; we know that our very existence depends on the grace and mercy of God. But we also proclaim that God has brought us together and has done so for a purpose beyond ourselves – for the salvation of the whole world. As Peter says, "Once we were outside the mercy, but now we have been brought under the mercy of God" (1Pet 2:10). And we exist to offer this mercy of God to every man and woman, and to bring them into communion within the sacramental experience of Christ in his Church.

Hope on the Horizon

This list of cultural woes could go on forever. But all is far from lost. The McCrindle report, a recent study of faith and belief in Australia,[61] showed that while only one in three Australians identify with a religion, more than half are open to change, and across the generations the most likely way they will open up to new spiritual insights is through an inspiring conversation. These are the conversations we need to create, not in a forceful way, but naturally as questions arise. More than half of Australians talk about spirituality or religion often or at least occasionally. While the dominant culture works against us, it seems more and more individuals quest for more than they presently experience. The younger generation are more likely to be open to change their current religious views than their elders. While giving religious institutions a miss they are spiritual seekers, recognising that the questions around the meaning and purpose of life are important to be addressed. Our response to the challenges of our age is not to throw up our hands in despair, but to be out amongst the people sharing their pain and their sorrows, listening to their struggles in life, and pointing them ever so gently towards Jesus, who will bring them the joy and peace for which their tormented lives yearn.

6
WITNESS OF LIFE

The McCrindle report shows that ordinary Australians value the Church and Christian organisations mainly for our work with the poor and disadvantaged.[62] Looking after the homeless, offering financial assistance and food relief programs, providing disaster relief assistance, looking after refugees and provision of aged care facilities all scored high in the estimation of unbelievers. This is good news in so far as the witness of these charitable works is noticed and has a positive impact. In addition, most of those who are warm towards Christianity, though not directly engaged, rate the Christians they know as caring, loving, and kind. This is further good news in that the witness of our personal lives is speaking to the unbeliever. However, non-Christians will quickly add to these positive qualities the charge of "judgemental" and "hypocritical". The biggest "belief blocker" is the Church's stance on homosexuality, and the biggest contributor to negative perspectives on the Church is the scandal of child sexual abuse amongst the leaders of the Church, including the cover-up by the pastors.

Our witness in today's world is obviously mixed in its reception. Undoubtedly the child sexual abuse crisis has done untold damage to how we are seen in current society. It has caused a major credibility crisis which will take years to restore. This has severely impaired our capacity to credibly proclaim the moral truths of the gospel, especially the Church's teaching on sexuality. But all is not lost. The Church has been necessarily humbled and purified through this crisis and we will eventually emerge as a more luminous sign of Christ in the world. We are a pilgrim people, holy because of God's presence with us, but sinful because of our own failings, always in need of renewal and reformation.

The environment in which we move will often be unfriendly and unfair in its evaluation of the Church. Much of this we must wear on the chin. Yet we are often subject to "bad press". While not blowing our own trumpet we could do a better communication job in describing our impact in the world. This reminds me of a young volunteer Catholic Church worker who on an international flight was sitting next to a highly educated sophisticated woman who in the course of conversation was attacking the Catholic Church because of widespread sexual abuse and undeclared wealth. He listened politely. After a while she asked him what he did for a living. Naturally he was reluctant to disclose that he worked for the Church. Instead he replied that he worked for an international non-State organisation which helps people. She was inquisitive and asked more about it. He informed her that this organisation is present in every country and runs programs helping build houses for the poor, caring for people with HIV/Aids, rescuing people from being victims of human trafficking, providing emergency relief in disasters, and financing a whole range of development projects, as well as running countless hospitals, schools and orphanages for the poor. "Wow," she said, "that is an amazing organisation". "Yes", he replied, "and that is just the beginning. In fact my organisation daily feeds, clothes, shelters and educates more people than any other organisation in the world". She was floored. "I have never heard of this. What is the name of this wonderful organisation?"

A Christian Subculture

In our situation in Australia where Christianity is now a subculture which is tolerated but is not valued by most, since in their minds it is irrelevant and outdated, the witness of our life will be critical. Pope Paul VI taught us that "for the Church, the first means of evangelisation is the witness of an authentically Christian life". He added most poignantly, "Modern man listens more willingly to witnesses than to teachers, and if he does listen to teachers, it is because they are good witnesses".[63] The Pope is telling us that it will be primarily by our way of life that we will evangelise the modern world. The witness of holiness of life, more than empty words will win our contemporaries. Earlier in the same exhortation Pope Paul asked us to imagine a Christian community which radiated faith in Christ, had an atmosphere of acceptance, sharing and caring for one another, a solidarity with the poor and the disadvantaged, a welcoming heart, and a joyful attitude to life.

> Through this wordless witness these Christians stir up irresistible questions in the hearts of those who see how they live: Why are they like this? Why do they live in this way? What or who is it that inspires them? Why are they in our midst? Such a witness is already a silent proclamation of the good news and a very powerful and effective one.[64]

Pope Francis has also often taught that the Church wins people to the faith not by proselytising but by attraction. By proselytising he means seeking to convert others by use of guilt, or psychological pressure, or by undue verbal persuasion. He suggests that particularly in countries such as Australia where the culture is hostile to the gospel we must win people by attraction. He likens this to the early Church in the context of the pagan Roman Empire. He advises us not to fall into moralistic preaching, seeking to show the superiority of the

Christian way of life. That just reinforces the existing prejudice that Christians are "judgemental". Facing a society like this, the testimony of our lives needs to be what attracts. Our lives should provoke curiosity, allowing the Spirit to move hearts to wonder, "Why do they do this?" People ask, "Are they crazy? Serving those who will not be able to survive, the disabled, the sick, in a culture which discards those who are no longer wanted or productive".[65] He says, questions will be provoked, and we must as Peter says, "always be ready to give an account of the hope that is within you" (1Pet 3:15).

As the First Christians

The Pope reminds us the first Christians converted the Roman Empire because of the radiant love they showed. We also must radiate love for every person, especially for our enemies. Love will win their hearts rather than argumentation and self-justifying proclamations. The impact of Christianity upon pagan Rome can be a lesson for us as we face a similar situation today. What impressed the Romans was how Christians lived. The Christians pushed back against the corruptions of a dying, death-dealing culture. They did not kill their unwanted babies. In Roman society female babies were seen as a burden, not a blessing and the majority of them were discarded. New born sons, if they showed any signs of deformity or weakness would also be killed or abandoned. Christians refused to conform to this social norm. They even went to the city gates and rescued the infants whom pagans had abandoned. This counter-cultural kindness confused but impressed the pagans.

Christians did not divorce, as Romans did; they were more likely to be chaste before marriage and faithful afterwards. The happiness and stability of Christian marriages was attractive. The ancient Romans saw in the home lives of the first Christians a way of love, respect and support for which their hearts longed. That intrigued them, and eventually they were drawn to conversion. Christianity was bringing about a quiet, substantial revolution of the prevailing culture. This is the essence of the new evangelisation. Christians rejected the cultural norms of the day – including infanticide, abortion, adultery, homosexual activity and the subjugation of women. They embraced a different way of life, a new way of seeing the human person. But they did not retreat into a ghetto mentality; they were engaged with the culture, transforming it from within by their uncompromising way of life.

Unlike the pagans Christians nursed the sick and dying. When epidemics occurred, most wealthy Romans would flee from the cities to protect themselves, leaving any sick relatives to die on the street. Christians did not live like the pagans. They were characterised by acts of mercy for those for whom they had no direct responsibility. They showed the face of the risen Christ in their actions before they spoke. Writing around the year 260, the Alexandrian bishop Dionysius gives an account of a mass epidemic:

> Most of our brother Christians showed unbounded love and loyalty, never sparing themselves and thinking only of one another. Heedless of danger, they took charge of the sick, attending their every need and ministering to them in Christ, and with them departed this life serenely happy; for they were infected by others by a disease, drawing on themselves the sickness of their neighbours and cheerfully accepting their pains….so that death in this form, the result of great piety and strong faith seems in every way the equal of martyrdom.[66]

Not only did Christians have a higher survival rate due to their care for one another during the plagues, but also the witness of their practical mercy won many pagans to join them.[67] Romans were inspired by their courageous love. In a world where suffering had no meaning, Christianity offered meaning. It offered comfort in sorrow, a refuge for those who were sick, a place in community where people experienced love, and care, especially for the deserted and discarded. Many pagans who survived the epidemics afterwards joined the Christians who had nursed them to health. In times of trial the pagan world was found wanting; in contrast Christianity shone as a beacon for the lost to find shelter.

Rather than flash marketing campaigns it will be the calibre of our lives that will ultimately appeal to the deadened hearts of our contemporaries. They will be attracted by what they see. The true way of the Beatitudes is the way of Jesus, and he is infinitely attractive to any human heart. We are to some degree failing in showing the true face of Jesus to people today, and in so far as the sign of the Church is ambiguous, people will not be drawn to Jesus.

A Divine Encounter

Some years ago a German tourist in her forties, who was travelling around Australia in a campervan, arrived in Canberra on a Sunday evening. As a sophisticated academic she had left the Catholic Church twenty years beforehand. But for some unaccountable reason, when she stopped at the information booth at the edge of the city, she felt a nostalgia for her Catholic background and asked where she could find a Catholic Mass. They directed her to the Cathedral. She arrived at the door of the Cathedral just in time for the start of the 7.00pm charismatic Mass. She said later that as she entered the Cathedral, which was full of people singing in praise of God, she was overwhelmed with a deep sense of God's love for her. During the Mass she wept copiously. Members of the community who were near her noticed and made contact at the sign of peace, and then afterwards invited her back to stay in an area where a number of community members live. Her campervan was found around the various community homes for a month or so. Before she left us she shared at a general gathering how much the welcome and love of the community had ministered to her. She felt she encountered Jesus in a new way through the love and friendship offered to her. She had discovered a living relationship with the risen Christ and had come back to her Catholic faith. She expressed her deep gratitude for this wonderful gift.

There is a touching sequel to the story. About six months later we heard back from Germany that she had contracted terminal cancer. One of the associates with the community travelled to be with her, and she died in the arms of her loving God. If our community existed only for that encounter, it would be enough. But thankfully there is so much more.

A Call to Holiness

Those who aspire to evangelise must first work on themselves. The first Christian book people read, even before the Bible, is usually ourselves. Our lives need to be good news. This is not an invitation to a "make over" in some superficial way to get the job done. Having worked with young people for years I am very aware that they are particularly quick to spot the fake; they naturally detect any scent of inauthenticity. I have learnt that before they will take hold of the words I speak, I must have convinced them that I am "for real". Not that we can embark on that as a project. We are either the "real deal" or we are not. They instinctively know which way it is, and react accordingly. People are truly attracted to Christ when he is incarnate in his friends. There is nothing more compelling than someone who really lives the Beatitudes. This is the secret of Pope Francis. He might drive some of the doctrinal pundits crazy because of his lack of precision at times in his off-handed conversations with the press; but he wins people because they know he loves them, regardless of their beliefs and values. He disarms even those who have opposing ideologies because he refuses to meet them firstly on that level; but simply as a highly respected fellow human being who is loved by God unconditionally, deserving of profound respect, and having inestimable dignity as a child of God. Pope John Paul II underlined this in words similar to Pope Paul VI:

> People today put more trust in witnesses than in teachers, in experience than in teaching, and in life and action than in theories. The witness of a Christian life is the first and irreplaceable form of mission.[68]

This need to be a witness of Christ is none other than a call to sanctity. As Pope John Paul II cryptically pronounced, "The Church today does not need any new reformers. The Church needs new saints".[69] Speaking to the young people for World Youth Day 2000 he called them to become "saints of the new millennium":

> Young people of every continent, do not be afraid to be the saints of the new millennium! Be contemplative, love prayer; be coherent with your faith and generous in the service of your brothers and sisters, be active members of the Church and builders of peace. To succeed in this demanding project of life, continue to listen to His Word, draw strength from the Sacraments especially the Eucharist and Penance. The Lord wants you to be intrepid apostles of his gospel and builders of a new humanity.[70]

In one short paragraph the Pope summed up our task. He tells us not to be afraid of becoming holy as God is holy. This can only happen through the Holy Spirit acting within us as a purifying fire and infusing us with a profound love for God and others. The Pope sets the agenda for a life of contemplation, and loving adoration of Jesus, who gradually changes us into his likeness; for a life of generous self-giving for others, listening constantly to His word and centering our lives around the sacraments of Reconciliation and the Eucharist. If we embark on this journey of discipleship we will gradually be transformed into the living image of Christ. When people meet us they will find Jesus reflected in the way we speak, the smile on our faces, and the way we relate to them with such love and compassion. We will then be authentic heralds of the gospel, and share in the work of changing our culture into a civilisation of life and love. We will be architects of a new humanity.

7
PROCLAIMING THE KERYGMA

The proclamation of the *kerygma* is at the heart of the new evangelisation. The term kerygma is a Greek word meaning "what is proclaimed". It is the catch-word to denote the core of the Christian message. It is centre of all that we are lovingly compelled to communicate to the world. Pope Francis sums the *kerygma* up as *"the saving love of God revealed in Jesus Christ"*. St Paul similarly gives a succinct expression of the *kerygma* in Romans: "Jesus, who was put to death for our sins, and raised to life for our justification" (Rom 4: 25). When the *kerygma* is proclaimed in the Spirit, people experience a living encounter with the risen Christ.

Peter at Pentecost

Peter's proclamation at Pentecost was simple and to the point. Under the anointing of the Holy Spirit he announced the *kerygma* with authority. This always has intrinsic power to change hearts. Speaking of Jesus, he cried out, "You killed him, but God raised him to life…all of us are witnesses to that…and what you see and hear is the outpouring of the Spirit…The whole house of Israel can be certain that God has made this Jesus whom you crucified both Lord and Christ" (Acts 2: 22-36). Some in the crowd would have known about Jesus, the Nazarene, being crucified. But this was now 50 days after the crucifixion. They would have been shocked that now Peter was proclaiming that Jesus was alive! He had already risen, but they did not know it.

Now as Peter spoke in the Spirit Jesus arose in their hearts. They became convinced he was alive. When Peter boldly proclaimed "You crucified and killed him", the crowd could have easily complained that they were not responsible. They were just coming to Jerusalem for the festival of Pentecost. But nobody complained about Peter's announcement. Why not? Because the Holy Spirit was convicting them of their sin. It was because of their sin that Jesus was nailed to the cross. As Isaiah said, "He was pierced through for our faults, crushed for our sins. On him lies a punishment that sets us free. By his wounds we are healed" (Is 53:5). *Our* sins also crucified the Son of God. We also need to be convicted of the truth. It was *our* sins that nailed him, but it was his love that kept him there. But, as Peter proclaimed to the people gathered in Jerusalem, "God raised him from the dead!" That is our hope. Peter was boldly proclaiming the overwhelming truth that "Jesus is Lord!"

Moved by his preaching the people cried out, "What must we do?" Convinced by the Holy Spirit that Jesus is Lord, they knew it meant a decision. Peter called them to repentance, faith and baptism in the Spirit. To recognise the Lordship of Jesus is to declare you belong to Jesus. It is to surrender your whole being into his loving hands and to trust your life to him. It is to accept that Jesus has every claim upon you; that he is Master of your life. It is an act of total submission that sets the soul free from captivity and brings you into a new intimacy with Jesus that sustains you through any trial or tribulation.

Jesus is Lord

Paul is a good example of this. After he had been blinded by an encounter with the glorious, risen Christ on the road to Damascus he spent three days in darkness. Then baptised by Ananias he was never the same again. Writing to the Philippians he says, "I believe nothing can outweigh the supreme advantage of knowing Christ Jesus, my Lord" (Phil 3:8). He was willing to accept the loss of every previous privilege and possession, as long as he had Christ and was given a place in him. The light of Pentecost reveals to us the truth of Jesus as Lord. Fr Raniero Cantalamessa, who had been a scholar in Christology at the University of Milan, testifies that it was not until he experienced the grace of the new Pentecost that he really came to know Jesus. While he had studied all that the Fathers of the Church had written about Jesus, and knew the theological controversies like the back of his hand, he had not yet really encountered Christ. He says,

> The discovery of Jesus as 'Lord' that came to me along with baptism in the Spirit wrought a great change that I would never have been able to achieve by myself alone. It seemed to me that I became able to see what lay behind Saint Paul's experience, when all at once he began to consider as 'disadvantage' all the things that before he had looked upon as 'advantages' he had enjoyed in life, and as "so much rubbish" everything other than "the supreme advantage of knowing Christ Jesus my Lord". I saw all at once what boundless gratitude, what pride and joy were hidden in that phrase of his, in that pronoun in the singular, "Christ Jesus *my* Lord".[71]

Fr Raniero goes on to say that there is a huge difference between the Christ you read about in books, and talk about in learned discussions, and the one whom we meet in reality. No wonder Pope Francis has called us all to a new level of reality:

> I invite all Christians, everywhere, at this very moment, to a renewed personal encounter with Jesus Christ, or at least an openness to letting him encounter them; I ask all of you to do this unfailingly each day. No one should think that this invitation is not meant for him or her.[72]

To proclaim Jesus is Lord in the time of the early Church was a dangerous thing indeed. It is an affirmation of the uniqueness of Christ. In the Creed we say "I believe in *one* Lord Jesus Christ" (cf 1 Cor 8:5-6). At that time the term "lord", *kurios* in the Greek, was used of the emperor. People were expected to bow before the emperor and burn incense before his effigy, acknowledging him as "lord". If they refused to do so the consequences were prison or death. In proclaiming "Jesus is Lord" Christians were refusing to bow in adoration before anybody but Jesus Christ, risen from the dead. The term *"kurios"* is the Greek translation of the ineffable Hebrew name *"YHWH"* from the Old Testament; they were proclaiming that Jesus is God. The newly born Christian faith was up against a world with many "gods" and "lords", yet they were ready to put their lives on the line for the proclamation that Jesus is Lord, the only true God. Paul quotes a hymn they used to sing in their liturgies, "God the father raised him from the dead and gave him a name which is above every other name, so that now at the name of Jesus every knee shall bow in heaven and in earth and in the underworld, and every tongue confess that Jesus Christ is Lord to the glory of God the Father" (Phil 2:9-11).

Heart of the Renewal

Unfortunately the sharpness of this fundamental proclamation was blunted quickly in the tradition. Already in the third century the title "Lord" was no longer used in the kerygmatic meaning. The term "Lord Jesus" became a name to refer to Christ but was largely emptied of its power. Often it was reduced to a description of his personage as "Our Lord". It is one thing to say "Our Lord Jesus Christ" and another to proclaim "Jesus Christ is our Lord!" However, in the late 1960s, just after the Council, with the new outpouring of the

Spirit, the proclamation on everyone's lips was "Jesus is Lord!" The Holy Spirit inspired songs and worship times focussed on this one proclamation. Since then we have been experiencing a revival of this kerygmatic enthusiasm. Jesus is not meant to be a figure to remember from the past, no longer a personage known from a distance, but a living person who is always present to us in the Spirit.

Paul tells us that "No one can say 'Jesus is Lord' unless he is under the influence of the Holy Spirit" (1Cor 12:3). With the new outpouring of the Spirit we are gaining a new freedom to proclaim the *kerygma*. At another time Paul says, "If you confess with your lips that Jesus is Lord and believe in your heart that God raised him from the dead you shall be saved" (Rom 10:9). In the light of the experience of Pentecost our proclamation, "Jesus is Lord" is more than lip service. It means we want Jesus to rule over everything – our job, our finances, our relationships, and every dimension of our life.

When we read the gospels we find that Jesus' whole ministry in word and action was to proclaim the "kingdom of God", which meant that God's loving rule was breaking into this world, and if we want fullness of life we need to submit to his reign over us through genuine conversion of heart. After the resurrection this proclamation *by* Jesus during his ministry becomes the proclamation *of* Jesus as Lord. It is the same message requiring the same response of repentance and faith. There can be no half-hearted response. The difference prior to Pentecost is that the disciples did not have the power of the Spirit to be able to respond whole-heartedly. After Pentecost, with the Spirit upon them, they now had the anointing for a new level of holiness and a new boldness to proclaim the good news. How much we need this Pentecost experience! Without it we are ill equipped for a life of discipleship and crippled in our attempts to evangelise.

Start from the Beginning

Under the grace of the new Pentecost we realise that we must start again. After 2,000 years of Christianity we have built up a huge edifice of magisterial teaching, liturgical celebration, theological reflection, manifold institutions, extensive laws to cover every situation, and a wealth of spirituality. This rich patrimony is the beauty of our Catholic experience. But in these days the Spirit is moving to call us back to the beginnings. At Vatican II there was a move to "return to the sources" for the sake of renewal. We went back to the scriptures and the Fathers of the Church to find a new vitality for our self-understanding as Church in the modern world. This has provided a totally new impetus for mission in the world today. This return to our origins must also recapture the simplicity of the kerygmatic proclamation of the good news. An image provided by Cantalamessa can help.

At the bow of a large ship there is a point which breaks through the sea first. This represents the proclamation of the *kerygma*, that Christ died for our sins and was raised for our justification, or more succinctly, "Jesus is Lord". But as the ship goes through the sea it leaves behind an ever widening wake, which is as it were expanding this initial point. At first there are the four gospels, written to explain the initial core of the message, and then the rest of the New Testament. Then came the Tradition of the Church with all its teaching, liturgy, theology, spirituality and laws. At this stage in history we have a wake from the ship with a vast expanse. If we are to evangelise the modern post-Christian world, where do we start? The huge arsenal of doctrine and plethora of institutions can be a hindrance if we are trying to reach those who have lost contact with the Church, and even for those who are still members but without much living personal faith. In our preaching we must start again at the beginning! It was the point of the bow of the ship which had the initial breakthrough at

Pentecost when Peter preached and 3,000 were converted. And it will be the same *kerygma* which will bring people to a personal encounter with Jesus today.

Stemming the Tide of Defection

Without this sharpness and clarity of proclamation of the gospel, and without the living personal encounter with Jesus that it brings, people will remain confused and disenchanted with the Church. Many are in fact defecting from the Catholic Church to Pentecostal or evangelical groups, not because they are necessarily scandalised by the Church but simply because they find the preaching of the word of God which is relevant to their lives, and have the meaning of scripture opened up for them. They also find a community of disciples which really believes what is preached and seeks to live it. Often when I meet these people I find that they simply fell in love with Jesus, who they had not previously been led to encounter, even though they were practising Catholics.

Our theology tells us this is nonsense, since every Eucharist is potentially the most personal living encounter with Christ available to us on this earthly journey. How could people who have been regular at Sunday Mass walk away? There was a serious disconnect between their liturgical life and their lived reality. To ignore the reality of their experience would be to our peril. They witness to the unexpressed hunger in so many to know the saving love of Jesus. They will not come to this personal faith unless Jesus is preached in the Spirit. As Paul said:

> All who call on the name of the Lord will be saved. But they will not call on his name if they do not have faith, and they will not have faith if they do not hear the word, and they will not hear the word unless they get a preacher, and they will not get a preacher unless one is sent. (Rom 10:14)

It is important to emphasise that faith does not simply come from some sort of cultural osmosis. As if you grow up in a Catholic family and you automatically become a believer. In a later chapter I intend to say something about the crucial role of culture in the transmission of faith. But the Catholic culture will be deficient for the task before us today if it does not have at its heart the proclamation of the *kerygma*. Otherwise we will continue to witness Catholic schools producing well-educated graduates, the vast majority of whom have little or no faith. We will continue to labour with parishes with well-meaning participants who have little or no motivation to do anything but maintain the status quo.

Missionary zeal only comes when there is a fire in the heart from a faith which has been personally awakened by kerygmatic preaching. Students in our schools and good people in our parishes have a hidden hunger for the gospel to be preached. Often they are not fully aware of this hunger since it is subliminal. But it can be awakened. It is as if they are like the Greeks who came to Philip requesting, "We want to see Jesus" (Jn 12:22). When the good news is proclaimed the Risen Christ himself is made present and he speaks; people "see Jesus" in the faith that is aroused. The Holy Spirit moves and persuades the listener, opening the heart. In the Acts when Paul was at Philippi he went down by the river and began to preach to some women. We are told by Luke that Lydia "listened to us, and the Lord *opened her heart* to accept what Paul was saying" (Acts 16:15). Our preaching the *kerygma* will open hearts, not due to our eloquence but due to the Holy Spirit at work in our listeners.

Unleashing the Hidden Energy of the Gospel

The burning question, which was voiced by Pope Paul VI, that keeps coming back to me, is "How in today's world can we unleash the hidden energy of the gospel in such a way that it can change the hearts of our contemporaries?"[73] I believe a vital part of the answer is in the proclamation of the *kerygma*. This is not only by spoken word, but also by drama, music and song, art and poetry. I remember when I had asked a young man to take part in the reading of the passion on Good Friday. He was to join with others in shouting out "Crucify him! Crucify him!" He told me later that as he did this he was overwhelmed with the truth that he had crucified Jesus by his sins and wept with tears of repentance. At weekends for young people often the turning point for many is the re-enacting of the passion of Jesus as they are touched deeply by the love the Saviour has for them and receive a grace to accept Christ as their Saviour and Lord.

When Paul wrote to the Galatians he was furious with them since they had submitted again to the ways of the Mosaic Law rather than live by faith in Christ. He says, "Are you people in Galatia mad? Has someone put a spell on you, before whose eyes Christ was publicly portrayed as crucified?" (Gal 3:1) Now Paul obviously had not presented a "passion play" for the Galatians. He had preached to them. This gives us a good insight into what and how he preached. He proclaimed Jesus crucified! Another translation says he gave "a plain explanation of the crucifixion of Jesus Christ". And Paul reminds them that it was not because of the Law that they received the Spirit, but because of his preaching the crucified Lord (Gal 3:2). The sort of preaching which has a transforming effect upon listeners is when Christ crucified and risen is proclaimed.

When Paul had preached to the Council of the Areopagus in Athens he had sought to meet them with some contemporary philosophy. But he had little success in convincing them. It seems this failure sharpened up his preaching. When he arrived at Corinth there was a new quality of fire in his message. He later reminds the Corinthians of how he came among them:

> As for me, brothers, when I came among you, it was not with any show of oratory or philosophy, but simply to tell you what God had guaranteed. During my stay with you, the only knowledge I claimed to have was about Jesus, and only about him as the crucified Christ.

He says he did not want to engage with them in philosophical debate, but only "by a demonstration of the power of the Spirit" (1Cor 2:1-5). When we preach Jesus crucified we can expect that the Holy Spirit will move powerfully amongst the people, just like at the first Pentecost. In this Spirit-filled mode of communication we are not in any way preaching ourselves, but holding up Christ to be honoured and adored. When we do this Christ himself speaks. As one great preacher said to me, "Whenever you stand up for Christ, he will stand up with you".

The Basic Content?

What is the content of the *kerygma*? What is the core message that needs to be proclaimed. I hesitate to give formulas, since there are a thousand ways to be creative in bringing this fundamental good news. In a previous book, entitled *Amazing Love*,[74] I attempted to give a thematic outline of this saving message, which is at the core of all Spirit-filled evangelisation. It is not easy to give a condensed version. I consider it more important for us to deepen in the mystery of Christ and his redemption of the world in all its many dimensions, and preach out of the reality of that experience. The danger is that we will settle for theological propositions, rather than witness to the truth of who Christ is for us now. Our proclamation has to be delivered in the Spirit and each time have a freshness and creativity provided by the Lord. However, if I was asked to make a quick summary of the content of the *kerygma* I would say something like this:

- God created us out of love to be in communion with him and with one another. His plan was for us to live in total harmony within ourselves and with one another. His love for us is total, unconditional and everlasting. We find our identity and worth in him, and our destiny is to be fully with him forever.
- Sin entered the world through Adam, and we all have sinned and fallen short of the glory of God. This has brought rupture to our relationship with God, with one another, within ourselves and with the whole of creation. It was impossible for us to restore this relationship with God which was broken by our disobedience
- "God sent his Son into the world, not to condemn the world but to save the world" (Jn 3:17). God became one of us so that by solidarity with us he could redeem us. He took upon himself the consequences of our sin, so that we could be set free. The cross is a sign of his infinite love for us. "What proves that God loves us is that Christ died for us". God the Father raised him from the dead. This is the source of our hope. We are set free from the power of sin and Satan, and given new life. "For all who are in Christ there is a new creation; the old is gone and the new is here" (2Cor 5:17).
- We need to say "yes" to what has been accomplished for us by Jesus and already applied to our lives through Baptism, when we were immersed into the death and resurrection of Christ. We need to repent of our sins, break with our old ways of living according to the ways of the world, and open ourselves to the saving power of Jesus Christ. We need to surrender to him as Lord of our lives

- We need to ask for the experience of a new Pentecost in our lives; to ask for the grace of our Baptism and Confirmation to be released more fully when we received the Holy Spirit for empowering in personal holiness and for bringing the good news of Jesus to others.
- All of this needs to be experienced within the community of believers and lead towards deeper Eucharistic communion.

8
GRACE AND MERCY

The self-sufficiency and self-reliant attitude prevalent in today's society plays into an endemic weakness in traditional Catholic culture. Not a few Catholics are still caught in the bind that they must earn their own way to heaven by good works. God will come to help them, but only to the extent that they attract his attention and win his favour by keeping their religious nose clean and staying out of too much trouble. We need to regain our belief in God's love, his grace and mercy. John says, "We are the ones who have put our faith in God's love for us" (1Jn 4:16). But many find this difficult. They are locked into an attitude akin to what Paul in his letters calls the "Law".

Paul insisted that keeping the Mosaic Law does not make you right with God. The Law can only show you how you have sinned, but it can't save you from sin. He was adamant that you can only attain salvation from sin by the sheer gift of God's grace, which was definitively released into the world by the death of Jesus on the cross and his resurrection into glory. We are made right with God by faith in what Jesus has accomplished for us on the cross, not by our unaided efforts to imitate his virtuous life from a distance. That is why Paul exclaimed, 'I am no longer living trying for perfection by my own efforts, the perfection that comes from the Law, but I want only the perfection that comes through faith in Christ, and is from God and based on faith".(Phil 3:9)

A Culture of Self-Help

Many popular books feed this cultural attitude of "self-help". They overlook the fundamental reality that our humanity is wounded by sin; that only by the salvation brought in Jesus Christ can we be healed and brought to new life. In the Church's theological tradition this fallacious way of thinking has been given the name Pelagianism. Pelagius was a Celtic monk who lived in Rome and Carthage in 390-418. He taught that Jesus was simply a good role model; we can imitate his virtue without needing the help of God. Jesus' death on the cross was merely a good example of love that we must follow. We could attain perfection by our own efforts if we work hard enough at the job.

St Augustine vigorously opposed this heresy by preaching the supremacy of God's grace. Augustine made it clear that we are wounded by original sin and can't do anything to correct the problem without the saving grace from the cross of Christ. This is why God came into the world. The heart of the kerygmatic proclamation is the famous text from John: "God so love the world that he gave his only Son, so that everyone who believes in him may not perish but may have eternal life" (Jn 3:16).

Later in Catholic tradition, since Pelagius had been discredited, another more subtle version arose called semi-Pelagianism. This was the idea that we must go a certain distance by our own efforts, using our own lights, and then at a certain point God will come to make up the rest. I once heard an eminent theologian say that in his opinion the majority of Catholics of our day are more or less semi-Pelagian. My own pastoral experience bears out the veracity of his off-handed comment. Behind much of the problem is a deficient understanding of God and his activity in our lives. It's as if God is in heaven waiting for us to get up enough "brownie points" to make the grade and then he will reward us accordingly. It is oblivious to the reality that

God has already come to save us in Jesus; that *he has loved us first*. As John says, "This is the love I mean; not our love for God, but God's love for us when he sent his Son to be the sacrifice that takes our sins away" (1Jn 4:10).

Rich in Mercy

God is all grace and mercy. Paul knew this because of his Damascus road experience. As a result of this gratuitous encounter with the reality and majesty of the Risen Christ he knew that all his pharisaical theology was now turned upside down. Even though he had been a murderer of Christians he had now experienced the sheer mercy of Christ upon him. He later writes to the Ephesians that God loved us so much he was "rich in mercy". Having found us in the mess of our sinful ways he should have rejected us, but instead he gave himself for us. "When we were dead through our sins, he brought us to life with Christ…and raised us up with him… it is by grace that you have been saved, through faith; not by anything of your own, but by a gift from God; not by anything that you have done, so that nobody can claim the credit" (Eph 2:4-9).

In the gospels Jesus challenges the Pharisees who were blinded by this "self-help" thinking. According to their perspective, a person was made righteous by fulfilling all the 613 prescriptions of the Law; those who could not do this were considered "sinners". Jesus did not attack the Law but rather this fallacious attitude which held an unreal ideal of perfection before ordinary people. When the Pharisees were aghast that he was eating with tax collectors and sinners, Jesus rebuked them, "It is not the healthy who need the doctor, but the sick. I did not come to call the virtuous but sinners" (Mk 2:17). This is why Pope Francis likes to call the Church a hospital for sinners rather than a club for the perfect. Jesus is rich in mercy.

Self-made religious virtue shuts people out from the mercy of God. Religion for them is a form of self-induced slavery rather than a source of freedom and healing. The older brother in the story of the prodigal son is locked into this "works will save" mentality. He has laboured hard on the farm all his life and resents the Father welcoming back his wayward brother. He cannot accept the Father's mercy, and in a self-righteous way shuts himself out from the joy of the Father's house. Those who have their Church activities under their control and maintain an upstanding moral life by much personal effort may still in fact have missed the heart of the gospel! If we have tried to make ourselves right with God, we can become self-righteous and isolated in our own self-made superior position. There's little joy in this. It becomes a miserable moralism, lacking in mercy towards others, and often ending up in disillusionment; inevitably we fall off the "ladder of perfection" that is impossible to climb in our own strength anyway.

Proclaim the Love of God

This semi-Pelagian mentality can be blown apart by the preaching of the *kerygma*. The "performance orientation" can be gently but firmly challenged by the truth of God's unconditional love. The Holy Spirit convicts hearts of the love of God, and opens us to a new encounter with Jesus. People need to hear a clear proclamation of the salvation won by Jesus and the wonderful promise of new life that comes through the Holy Spirit. "For all who are in Christ Jesus there is a new creation. The old is gone and the new is here" (2Cor 5:17). We all need to hear the *kerygma* proclaimed again and again, especially because of the pathological elements of our popular Catholic heritage, and also because of the broad social environment which promotes individualistic self-sufficiency. Pope Francis says:

This first proclamation is called 'first' not because it exists at the beginning and can then be forgotten or replaced by other more important things. It is first in a qualitative sense because it is the principal proclamation, the one which we must hear again and again in different ways, the one which we must announce one way or another through the process of catechesis, at every level and moment.[75]

Ministers of the Gospel

This "*we* can do it" mentality does not only paralyse one's personal journey towards God, but also sucks the energy out of ministry in Catholic parishes and schools. Good teachers and pastors become disillusioned. Initial ideals are crushed and they develop a deadly cynicism, no longer expecting anything worthwhile to happen, and often on the edge of "burn-out". Teachers who are looking for results feel little is attained, frustrated by difficult students in the school, and their inevitable rebellion and unbelief. Those working in parishes can similarly feel loaded with demands beyond their capacity, and have a sinking feeling that the game is slowly being lost, as the pews show no signs of filling up again, and relatively few faithful ones keep the parish functioning. The problems we face are real enough. But maybe we need a revolution in our thinking about how to approach them. Could it be that many good people in the Church are burning themselves out because they are trying to do a supernatural task by natural means? Could it be that we need to rely more upon the Holy Spirit?

Teachers can be so focussed on better methods of pedagogy and methodologies in teaching that they miss the main issue. Professional excellence is a good thing, but of itself it will not provide what we need. The Catholic school exists to evangelise. It does not just *have* a mission. It *is* mission. But it is not a mission like any social club or society dedicated to doing good. Often the mission statements in foyers of schools tend to read like that. No, the mission is to bring the good news to the students and make them disciples of Jesus. This cannot be achieved without the Holy Spirit. We need to learn again to be dependent upon God. Jesus said, "I am the vine, you are the branches. Those who abide in me and I in them, will bear fruit in plenty; for cut off from me *you can do nothing*" (Jn 15:5). Strong words! He did not say cut off from me you will limit your effectiveness. Rather, cut off from me you can do *nothing*. Why? Because that is the sort of ministry in which we are engaged. It relies upon God! Without him it is useless.

Prayer and the Holy Spirit

Once when I was visiting the Congregation for Doctrine and Faith, together with other leaders of the Renewal, we had a blessed meeting with Cardinal Ratzinger, who later became Pope Benedict XVI. The Cardinal listened to various people brief him about what was happening in the Charismatic Renewal on each continent. After listening to these reports he told us that usually when people came to his Dicastery they brought bad news. He thanked us for bringing good news instead. Then he shared that, when he was a young priest, he used to think that all we needed for the renewal of the Church was more professionalism, better programs, and well planned outreaches. But he continued, "Now I know what we need most is prayer and the Holy Spirit". I was impressed by his humility and the wisdom of those words. They apply to every Catholic parish and every Catholic school. We need more prayer and more of the Holy Spirit!

I was convinced of this myself after about twelve years as a priest. During that time I had gone through some disillusionment, and had tried to remedy the issue by further graduate studies. But the secret to the renewal of the Church still eluded me. I worked hard for renewal but it seemed the People of God were acting not so much as God's *chosen* people, but as God's *frozen* people! My question was, "How could we de-frost the Church?" I was inclined to think the problem was with the people, not realising it was with me. I found the answer when attending a priest's charismatic retreat. The preacher, Fr Tom Forrest, a Redemptorist based in Rome, had a simple pitch. He told the hundred priests on the retreat, "You need to be able to say three words." I was keen to know what these words were, since I was hungry for answers. After a dramatic pause for effect, he gave the key words: "I CAN NOT". I was at that stage in ministry when I instinctively knew this was the truth. Ministry in my own strength was not working. Failure followed me everywhere, together with the accompanying frustration. If I continued in this vein, "burn out" would be inevitable. Fr Tom continued, "You need to be able to say one more word: 'YES'." This means "Yes, God, *you* can do it!" He encouraged us to join our "yes" to that of the Blessed Virgin Mary. When faced with what was impossible, Mary asked how could this happen. She was told that the Holy Spirit would come upon her and she would be overshadowed with the power of the most High God. Without hesitating she made her "yes", surrendering to the power of Holy Spirit. This is the secret for the renewal of the Church's mission.

If Jesus has established his Church, and parishes and schools are his instrument for bringing the good news, how could they be failing? The problem can't be on the Lord's side. He has promised to be with his Church. The problem must be with us. We sense this and work harder, but inwardly many sense there must be something we are missing. What could be the missing key for ministries in the Church to flourish? The answer is simple. His name is Jesus; without him we can do nothing. We cannot undertake a supernatural mission with only natural resources.[76] I know that is a stark statement and maybe an unfair judgement on some. But I make it to help kick-start the reader into a deeper dependency on God. The only way we can save Catholic education, and the only way parishes can fulfil their mission, will be through radical dependence on the risen Christ and the power of his Holy Spirit. This is the fuel needed to set hearts ablaze; this is the fuel needed to energise and empower our ministries. This is the way of the new evangelisation – humble dependence on God.

9
A PROCESS OF CONVERSION

The whole aim of the new evangelisation, and the proclamation of the *kerygma*, is to arouse a deeper conversion in its recipients. Pope Paul VI insisted that evangelisation aims to attain the spiritual renewal of individuals:

> The purpose of evangelisation is precisely this interior change, and if it had to be expressed in one sentence the best way of stating it would be to say that the Church evangelises when she seeks to convert solely through the divine power of the message she proclaims.[77]

Pope John Paul II in a similar vein said, "The proclamation of the word of God has Christian conversion as its aim: a complete and sincere adherence to Christ and his gospel through faith".[78] Conversion involves a breaking with the old way of life which was not under the rule of Christ and then subjecting one's whole life under him and his ways. It is the grace of a new encounter with Jesus, the risen Lord and a surrender of one's life to him.

A Change of Heart

The New Testament word for conversion is *metanoia*, a complete change of direction, a total change of mind and heart, a breaking with the way of the kingdom of darkness and an embracing of the kingdom of God. It is often translated as repentance; under the grace of God a person acknowledges their faults and makes a decision to turn from sin and to turn to Christ as their Saviour. In Catholic parlance we do not understand this as one moment of grace alone when a person hears the word and experiences a change of heart. Rather it is an on-going process in life. However, there are decisive moments in anyone's personal history when we have allowed the word of God to pierce our hearts and yielded more fully to God's saving power. The Catholic Catechism says, "Interior repentance is a radical reorientation of our whole life, a return, a conversion to God with all our heart, an end of sin, a turning away from evil, with repugnance toward the evil actions we have committed".[79] This comes about by the action of the Holy Spirit. As we look upon the crucified Christ who has been pierced through for our sins (Jn 19:37; Zech 12:10) we have revealed to us the immensity of God's love and mercy. "Our heart is shaken by the horror and weight of our sin and begins to fear offending God by sin and being separated from him". We are given the strength to start afresh.[80]

This conversion of heart is a life-long process; again and again we need to be subjected to the proclamation of the *kerygma* through preaching, drama, song, electronic media, liturgical celebration, which will call our hearts to a deeper response to God's love. At every step of the journey we need to ask ourselves the question: How much have we allowed ourselves to be converted to the Lord? To what depth has it happened? The conversion of many can be quite shallow. They manifest religious practice but not the depth of interior change that is meant to happen. Their life is not showing the fruits of the Spirit of love, joy, peace, patience, kindness and self-control (Gal 5:22). They are somewhat compromised in their hearts. They are resistant to truly living the demands of the gospel of Jesus. They live with divided hearts. Genuine conversion means putting the old self to death and putting on the new self in Christ (Eph 4:17-24).

Three Dimensions of Conversion

There are three mutually interrelated dimensions of conversion. Firstly, there is intellectual conversion. This is a growing conviction of the truths of the faith and a readiness to adhere to them with fidelity. This happens under the illumination of the Holy Spirit. Secondly, there is moral conversion. This means not only agreeing with the moral teachings of the Church, but freely changing one's behaviour to conform to this teaching. This is not an attempt to obey the commandments in a self-sufficient way, but under the grace of God and by his power. Thirdly there is spiritual conversion which is when we are so touched by the Spirit that we fall in love with God, and experience him as Saviour and Lord.

Sometimes, through effective apologetics, people may be convinced of the truths, but not yet feel capable of living the moral life. St Augustine was like that. Under the preaching of Ambrose he knew Christianity was the truth but his lustful desires kept him in bondage until in a grace-filled moment he received a sovereign gift from God. Often young people today are living disordered moral lives, and may be quite ignorant about doctrine, but when they encounter Jesus through a spiritual experience on a weekend or retreat they find a new insight into the truth and a new conviction and power to change their errant behaviour. Prior to this new infusion of grace a thousand sermons and moral instructions would have fallen on deaf ears. But now God's Spirit has broken through the darkness and new possibilities for change occur.

A New Environment

The new evangelisation means not only the initial proclamation which brings first stages of conversion, but an on-going work of discipleship in a community of faith. Within a supportive community the newly converted can deepen in what is as yet a fragile reality. Conversion has been likened to the transplanting of an ailing shrub from one environment to the next. All the roots in the old toxic and threatening environment need to be gently but firmly taken out with the shrub, and then it needs to be put into the new environment which is more favourable towards its growth. All the roots that have been feeding on the old environment which shaped the old self need to be pulled up. Our roots need to be put down firmly into a new environment, which can provide nourishment for our lives and foster the growth of our new self in Christ. This new environment is a Christian community which is living a whole new way of life in Christ. Pope John Paul II, referring to new converts to the faith, wistfully makes the following observation:

> Such converts bring with them a kind of new energy, an enthusiasm of faith, and a desire to see the gospel lived out in the Church. They would be greatly disappointed if, having entered the ecclesial community, they were to find a life lacking in fervour and without signs of renewal! We cannot preach conversion unless we are converted anew every day.[81]

Within the new environment of the Christian community new converts need to learn to break with the ways of the world, do business with sinful attitudes, work on overcoming the power of the flesh and resist the temptations of the devil. They also need to work on developing a life of virtue under the influence of the Holy Spirit.[82] All of this takes time, and we need to be realistic that the journey of most disciples is punctuated with failures. When this happens they will need someone at their side to help them not to fall into discouragement, but to repent, and to gently rise up again and keep persevering in the ways of God. Personal transformation is a life-long task and the main principle is to keep going regardless of what happens, and never to give up.

Importance of the Sacraments

Catholic evangelisation always involves initiation into full sacramental life in the Church. We do not just call people into a personal relationship with Jesus in isolation from his Church. For Paul, to come to know Jesus means to be incorporated into his Body. Those who say they believe in Christ but want nothing to do with the Church are not living according to the New Testament teaching. When Paul experienced the risen Christ on the Damascus road he heard the words, "Saul, Saul, why are you persecuting me?" Paul could have protested, "But I am not hurting you; I am persecuting your followers". But in the three days of darkness he endured before his sight was restored to him no doubt Paul pondered these words. To touch the community of Christians was to touch Christ, because we have our life together in him. We are the Body of Christ. We are baptised into his Body. God does not bring salvation to us individually but through a community. Incorporation into the Body of Christ is integral to the evangelisation process.

When we talk about our conversion being a life-time journey this will include receiving God's life through the sacraments. In contrast, an evangelical Protestant sees the goal of evangelisation as leading someone to belief in Christ alone; once the person expresses a prayer of personal commitment to Jesus as one's Saviour and Lord then all is accomplished. But for Catholics this is just the beginning; a very important initial step, but there is so much more to come. To embrace Jesus is to embrace his Body, the Church, and all that goes with Catholic communion. Usually in the evangelical Protestant world that initial commitment establishes you as "saved", once and for all. But the Catholic perspective is that this crucial step of heartfelt commitment to Christ, while being a "yes" to all that Jesus has done for you, is but one step on a long journey of appropriating the saving love of Christ in our lives. When my Protestant friends ask me, "Are you saved, brother?" I respond, "Yes, I *have* been saved, I *am being* saved, and I trust I *will be* saved in the end". In other words, I am in process; as yet unfinished. We live a sacramental life, constantly opening up our lives to the saving power of Jesus, guaranteed for us in these beautiful moments of regular encounter with him.

The other side of this issue is the unfortunate reality that many Catholics who have benefitted from receiving the sacraments for years have not yet been given the opportunity of making their "yes" to God's saving love through an explicit commitment to him in a personal and meaningful way. As discussed earlier, the grace of the sacraments can only bear fruit in our lives to the extent that we are open and surrendered of heart for this to happen. Once Catholics have heard the word in a new way as an adult and responded in repentance and faith, they will find a whole new love for Jesus in the sacraments and a joyful expectation of their fruitfulness in their lives.

Centrality of the Eucharist

Eucharist by definition is the joyful proclamation of Jesus crucified until he comes again. It is a profoundly evangelical reality; as is the Church who celebrates it. The Eucharist is a word-event in which the crucified and risen Christ is made present for all. This is the sacrament that makes present the sacrifice of Jesus given for the salvation of the world. It is directed outwards to all men and women. In the Eucharistic prayer we pray that the fruits of the sacrifice will be experienced by all, but then we move out as a people to actively bring this gift of salvation to as many as possible. At the end of the Mass the celebrant in the name of Jesus and his church sends the participants forward with the words, *"Ite missa est"*, "Go you are sent". The name Mass (*Missa*) is taken from this dismissal formula. We are the people who are "sent". Jesus said to his apostles on Easter morning, "As the Father has sent me, so I am sending you!" Another possible dismissal the priest can use is, "Go, and announce the gospel of the Lord!" Everything is geared towards joyfully going forth, preaching the good news that we have a loving Saviour who has redeemed us and is our hope. As Pope Benedict has reminded us, "we cannot approach the Eucharistic table without being drawn into mission, which beginning with the heart of God, is meant to reach all people".[83]

Pope John Paul II wrote, "The Eucharist thus appears as both the *source* and the *summit* of all evangelisation."[84] When we celebrate Eucharist we are expressing who we are as a people and we are seeking to become more deeply who we are. An authentic Eucharistic Church is a missionary Church. It is simply a matter of being true to ourselves. In the Eucharist we experience a profoundly personal encounter with the risen Christ still carrying his wounds. There is nothing more beautiful for the human heart than to be surprised again by the power of God's word proclaimed in the Eucharist and by receiving the incarnate Word himself in Holy Communion. This living encounter with Jesus impels us to share joyfully with others the light, hope, and freedom which he brings to human hearts. As Pope Benedict observes, "The more ardent the love for the Eucharist in the hearts of the Christian people, the more clearly will they recognise the goal of all mission: *to bring Christ to others.*"[85]

Within the Eucharistic Community

It is helpful to be able to position the actual Eucharistic celebration within the overall process of evangelisation. If we were to draw up a rather stylised pattern of the way a person is evangelised, we could identify three stages. Firstly, a time of initial evangelisation which is achieved largely through individual witness of members of the community who are on fire with the love of Jesus, living closely with people and involved in their daily lives, full of compassion and ready to listen to the heart-aches they have, supporting them in practical ways and encouraging them in initial steps of faith. At this stage the witness of the community itself is crucial. It is simply a matter of saying to a friend, "come and see!" We need to be confident they will discover a new way of life witnessed in the relationships and the manner of living of the Christian community. Whether it is someone returning to the Church, or an unchurched person who has a curiosity and openness to the Church, it's good to invite them to Mass. They begin to experience the liturgy which in itself has power to move people at a subliminal level below consciousness.

The second phase is the time of being soaked in the proclaimed word of God which is aiming towards conversion of heart. Here it is crucial that the newcomer hears the *kerygma* preached, the fundamental proclamation of the saving love of God made visible in Jesus crucified. At Mass they will hopefully hear *kerygmatic* preaching, but there may also be other contexts, such as a home-based prayer meeting, an organised rally, an Alpha program, A Life in the Spirit seminar, set aside for this purpose. At this time they have the opportunity to make a personal response of commitment to the Lord.

In the third phase the person is ideally guided in a one to one relationship with one of the members of the community. This is a time of deepening in personal conversion to Jesus. Having responded to the gospel message the person has encountered Jesus as Saviour and Lord and is now developing in a personal relationship with Jesus through solid catechesis, learning about the scriptures and the teachings of the Church, and dipping into other audio or visual sources for feeding. It is a time of being fully incorporated into the life of the local Church. The person will learn more about the meaning and purpose of the Eucharist and learn how to consciously and actively participate in the celebration. He or she will also discover the wonder of Eucharistic adoration. The daily food of the Eucharist and regular periods of adoration of Jesus in the Blessed Sacrament provide a fire within the heart, a love that propels them forward to want to share this gift with others.

10
THE GIFT OF PREACHING

In contemporary society "preaching" is almost a dirty word. "Don't preach to me!" is the often-heard reproach. People are antagonistic towards any attempt to be "preached at". Preachers ignore this reality to their peril. Part of the problem is that people don't want to be told to do anything that might interfere with their own chosen life-plans. They also react against anyone claiming to have certainty about complex life-issues. Both these attitudes derive from the individualistic, relativism of the age. But I suggest the main problem may not be with the mind-set of the society but with the preachers themselves? Too often we can appear to be "preaching at" people, rather than communicating the good news of God's love.[86] In other words we value the message that we preach more than those to whom we preach. We do not communicate with love and respect, but with what appears to others as a self-righteous superiority. The first task of the preacher is to win over the listener by not "speaking *at*" them, but by "speaking *to*" them with love. Good preachers will have the heart of the Good Shepherd. The love of Christ will radiate through their body language, tone of voice and style of delivery. Good preachers obviously care for those to whom they are speaking. They will certainly have an urgency for the salvation of those to whom they are preaching, but there will not even be a tinge of the classic stereotypical "bible-bashing" that alienates people and is a disservice to the gospel.

An Icon of Christ

People read the preacher first.[87] We are to be icons of Christ. As a preacher, I am the first message people receive. I am a symbol that says more than my words can express. If people perceive me as superior, condescending, and dogmatic they will shut down. But if they perceive me as a fellow-traveller, in solidarity with them, sharing their weaknesses, and fallible, they will be more open to listen. We proclaim the gospel out of our weakness, not out of our strength. By this I do not mean that we are wishy-washy about what we preach. We must have a passionate conviction of the truth of God's salvation in Jesus Christ. We speak the truth in love. If we are ablaze with the fire of God's love, what we speak will ignite a fire in those who are listening. However, for authenticity we should only speak what we have incarnated within ourselves. Otherwise the word is experienced as abstract ideas rather than a lived reality. We should be reluctant to preach anything we have not personally experienced. There needs to be continuity between the gospel message and the person. Jesus himself was the perfect image of the message he preached.

Preaching is an act of loving communication – the love of God flowing through the renewed person of the preacher to those who are listening. We aim not to separate but to win by love. For this reason preachers should not be afraid to share of themselves. While the basic content of the preaching must be the *kerygma*, it helps to relate personal experiences. This facilitates a more loving communication. The preaching is less didactic and more relational. Yet a warning is appropriate. Don't fall into the trap of overdoing the sharing, so that your listeners get sick of your mawkish self-revelations that would best be kept private. The personal sharing should help the proclamation of the gospel. Otherwise it is inappropriate. Paul put it plainly, "For it is not ourselves that we are preaching, but Christ Jesus, the Lord" (2Cor

4:5). Nevertheless if we are willing to be vulnerable and share our own struggles in life this can open people up and help them identify with the message we preach.

An Act of Prophecy

Preaching is also a prophetic act. The question to ask before preaching is "What does the Lord want to say to the hearts of his people?" We need to enter into the word-event prayerfully; listening and waiting upon the Lord.[88] We want to speak the word for this moment for this particular group of people. We need the inspiration of the Holy Spirit.

In our preparation we ask the Holy Spirit to give his word, but also in the act of preaching itself we need to rely upon the Spirit. Sometimes the Spirit will prompt us to move in a whole different way than planned. At Pentecost the apostles received the "gift of utterance", and today's preacher needs to ask for the same. Anthony of Padua, the great Franciscan preacher, speaks of this gift:

> The apostles, for their part, spoke as the Holy Spirit gave them utterance. Blessed is he who speaks under the inspiration of the Holy Spirit and not as his own human spirit suggests. There are some who speak from their own spirit; they pilfer the words of others and pass them off as their own, taking the credit themselves…
>
> Let us speak then as the Holy Spirit gives us utterance. Let us ask him humbly and earnestly to bestow his grace on us, so that we fulfil the day of Pentecost…let us ask for a keen sentiment of contrition, and for fiery tongues to profess the true faith.[89]

Paul distinguishes between preaching (the announcement of the *kerygma*) and teaching (*didache*, which presents doctrines, ethical norms and correct conduct for the believer).[90] Preaching brings to conversion; teaching brings on-going formation. Preaching births or rebirths communities in faith; teaching helps deepening in discipleship. Both are essential for Christian community. Without preaching of the *kerygma* faith does not blossom. Just as it was the secret to the birthing of the Church at the beginning, so it is the secret to the rebirthing of the Church in our day. Faith flowers only in the presence of the proclamation of Jesus crucified. Faith comes from hearing. It is not caught automatically, but from listening to the *kerygma* proclaimed. As Paul says:

> Everyone who calls on the Lord will be saved. But they will not cry out to him unless they believe in him, and they will not believe in him unless they hear the word, and they will not hear the word unless they get a preacher, and they will not get a preacher unless one is sent…So faith comes from what is heard and what is heard comes from the word of Christ. (Rom 10:13-17)

Proclaiming the *Kerygma*

The germinating nucleus of all that is said in preaching must be the proclamation of Jesus' death and resurrection. As I have emphasised in the previous chapter this nucleus is like the ploughshare, the sword-like point in front of the plough that first breaks the earth and allows the plough to mark out the furrow and turn over the earth. After this first breakthrough there is much to be done, but without the initial thrust what follows can be somewhat confused and ineffective. If we teach through catechism and sacramental initiation without also proclaiming the *kerygma*, we cannot attain the level of conversion necessary for people to sustain regular commitment to the sacraments and to bear the yoke of the commandments.

The majority of Catholic people can be likened to the two disciples on the road to Emmaus. Even though Jesus was walking with them they did not recognise him. When he asked them what they were talking about, they told him all the facts of the *kerygma*, but they had not grasped their meaning. They needed someone to proclaim the true meaning of these events that had occurred in Jerusalem, the death and resurrection of Jesus. As Jesus did so their hearts burned within them. Many Catholics likewise know the facts of the *kerygma* which they have learnt from their Catechism classes. But they need a preacher to proclaim to them the significance of these events. Then their hearts also will burn within them. When kerygmatic preaching is released more fully in the Church, we will see a dramatic change to the Catholic spiritual landscape.

Preaching for a Response

Often in the Church we hear a call for commitment without first preaching the gospel and leading them into a new release of the Holy Spirit. This leaves people heavily burdened in shame, guilt and a sense of inadequacy. They have not found the power of the Spirit which comes when we open up to respond to the gospel message. They are left powerless; bereft of the grace they need to do what is asked of them. When people surrender to the power of the Holy Spirit they experience a new freedom to live as they believe they are called to live. Without the new outpouring of the Holy Spirit they flounder in their attempts to follow the way of the Lord, and can easily fall into disillusionment and feel resigned to failure. Kerygmatic preaching aims at conversion, but does not call people to change without offering them the means by which to make that change.[91] They are called to a response, a real "yes" to God at work in their personal lives. As they experience a personal new Pentecost they have a new hope in their hearts. As Paul says, "this hope is not deceptive because the love of God has been poured into our hearts by the Holy Spirit" (Rom 5:5)

When the word of God is preached in the Spirit there is an anointing on the word spoken. The heart of the listener is opened by the Spirit. The preacher needs to be sensitive to this and draw upon the gift of wisdom to know what the Lord is doing at that time. He or she will always preach for a response. Of course, in general terms the response will happen over one's whole life and be lived out in many different circumstances. Nevertheless the evangelical preacher will be listening to the Spirit as he or she preaches, seeking the wisdom of God as to what the Lord is doing right now with these people. What will be the appropriate response? If we believe in the power of the word we must believe that God is doing something right now as we proclaim. Of course we will never be able to tap into everything that is happening since God's ways are not our ways. Yet he will prompt us to invite some sort of response.

The preacher needs to seek to move under the "anointing" of the Holy Spirit.[92] This is a grace given for this moment. We need to deliberately place ourselves under that anointing, and trust the Lord with the flow and direction of the event. Sometimes the anointing is more intense than others. The word of God has intrinsic power. The Hebrew "*dabar*" means the word in action. When the prophets spoke they expected something to happen (cf Is 55:10-11). When Jesus spoke there was power in his words: demons fled, people were healed, and many came to repentance. The people were astonished and knew there was a huge difference between the way he spoke and the way the scribes spoke. When Jesus spoke things happened (cf Mk 1:27). The scribes explained the Law, Jesus proclaimed the kingdom. He was not just imparting information or giving moral instruction or entertaining or simply giving an inspiring oration. He preached for conversion, *"metanoia"* in the Greek; meaning a change of heart, a radical "turn around" in their attitudes and actions. An effect was expected from the proclamation. The response was part of the word-event. The same applies for us as we preach the *kerygma*. When we do so in the Spirit we can expect a response, and call it forth from our listeners.

The Language of Preaching

The language of instruction is not the appropriate discourse for preaching. Rather to preach is to announce with deep conviction the word of God for these people now. The Catholic people in these days are crying from within, "We want to see Jesus" (Jn 12:22). They are looking for a preacher who will speak in such a way that they encounter Jesus speaking to them. They want to know Jesus. They want the preacher to reveal Jesus to them. They are seeing the new life and hope that only Jesus can bring. For this sort of proclamation, like Jesus who used parables, we don't use prosaic language of concepts, ideas and propositions. Rather we seek to use the language of symbol, imagery and story. Rather than giving eloquent speeches or heavy theological concepts, evangelical preaching speaks in such a way that the simplest person can understand, and it uses symbolic language and word pictures.

The language of preaching appeals primarily to the imagination and to the "symbolic consciousness".[93] The knowledge that symbols give is not cold, abstract information: it is "participatory knowledge". It is "poetic simple" language, which moves at a subliminal level. It is language that is evocative and transformative which shatters settled reality and evokes new possibility in the listening assembly. Hans Urs von Balthasar affirms "God needs prophets in order to make himself known, and all prophets are necessarily artistic. What a prophet has to say can never be said in prose."⁹⁴ When we are preaching we are often telling stories, sharing experiences, and announcing the fundamental Christian story in image-laden biblical language. With our stories relevant to the message we will be often touching peoples' "funny bone" since laughter has a way of relaxing our listeners, winning them with humour, putting them "off guard" and making them more receptive as we announce the good news.

Who Can Preach?

Some of the best preachers I have heard are lay people. The gift has especially appeared in a fresh new way under the anointing of the Spirit in the new ecclesial movements and new communities. This is an exciting time for the Church. Clerics need not feel threatened by this. The Spirit gives his charisms as he wills. Of course, the Eucharistic homily is the responsibility of the priest or deacon and cannot be delivered by a lay person. This is because it is a liturgical act, interpreting the readings of the day, performed by the ordained minister acting in the person of Christ as Head of the Church. Pope Francis dedicated a sizable portion of his exhortation *The Joy of the Gospel* to the homily; keen to help priests make their homilies heart to heart communication to their people setting hearts on fire because they open listeners to a living encounter with the Risen Christ. The importance of the homily in the life of the Church cannot be over-emphasised. The renewal of homiletic preaching in a kerygmatic mode is key for Church renewal.

We have seen that in the early Church it was common practice for lay people to participate in the Lord's commission to preach in the various circumstances of their daily life. However, by the fifth century lay preaching had become severely restricted. Pope Leo the Great (440-461) strictly forbad lay people from any form of public preaching.[95] Through the Middle Ages there was some relaxing of this prohibition but, generally speaking, preaching was held as the reserve of the clergy. The bishops were seen to have the full apostolic mandate to preach and they communicated this by way of grants of permission to the clergy, and occasionally to inspired laity or religious, such as friars and monks and significant evangelical figures. The fundamental reason for tight control was the unfortunate heretical preaching that often arose when lay movements began. A classic example was at the time of Francis of Assisi, who as a layman had received permission to give exhortations to the faithful. A similar grant was given to a spiritual lay leader, Peter Waldo, whose movement unfortunately became progressively ant-clerical and hostile to the Church.

While there was some limited provision for lay people preaching in the market place, there was a consistent prohibition on lay people preaching in a church building.[96] This held firm until the 1970s when the first modifications in law began. By this new provision lay people, who could relate well to children, could help speak in a children's liturgy, giving the priest a welcome break. Then the new Code of Canon Law (1983) acknowledged explicitly the lay participation in the ministry of the word. The Code allowed lay people to preach in a church or oratory if circumstances warranted it (Canon 766). However, it was clear that the homily in a Eucharistic celebration could never be entrusted to the non-ordained. This has rightly been non-negotiable.

While there is no room for lay preaching in the Mass we are witnessing a surge of lay preaching in other settings. In schools, church halls, conferences, prayer meetings, rallies, new ecclesial communities, evangelising teams, retreats and many other situations lay people are proclaiming the word powerfully. This is a wonderful new fruit of the new evangelisation under the new outpouring of the Spirit in our days. In addition to these more formal settings lay preaching is especially found in a multitude of life's contexts – in the home, at work, in the gym, at university, with friends and neighbours, with strangers on public transport. In a secularised world, when only 10% of Catholics are in the church on Sunday, and we have seemingly lost contact with the vast majority of our youth and young adults, evangelising in these informal settings is crucial.

The core style of evangelistic preaching in these contexts is casual, relational, and sharing. It focusses on a personal encounter with Christ.[97] It avoids religious jargon, seeks to meet people where they are, and brings the good news of Jesus into that situation. Because people today think religion has nothing to do with real life, this sort of encounter seeks to help people see that Jesus does make a difference. This is best done by personal witness rather than by appearing to be too dogmatic. Sharing our own personal testimony adapted to a person's needs engages them more readily than simply announcing the gospel message alone. We speak the word into the hearts of people in a non-threatening way in the midst of casual, friendly dialogue about life and its many questions and anomalies. People are free to accept or reject our testimony but they have to face the truth that it actually did happen. We are a living witness to the saving love of God in Jesus, incarnate in our own lives.

The Power of Testimony

Often we have the opportunity of sharing our testimony without necessarily preaching as such. This can happen in casual encounters on public transport, having coffee with a friend, or in more formal settings such as a youth group, a rally, or even during the liturgy, when the priest invites a lay person to share. Sharing about how you came to know and follow Jesus is possibly the most effective way of conveying the good news. Each person has a personal story which is unique and naturally interesting to those who are curious or inquisitive about the faith. The beauty about personal testimony is that it is indisputably true. Arguments can be disputed, but the real lived experience of another cannot be so easily dismissed.

When sharing one's testimony it is important not to beef it up to sound fantastic beyond the simple truth. Honesty is the key. It needs to be down-to-earth, true to life, free of religious jargon, simple, clear, and not too long. A testimony simply witnesses to how God's love has touched your life through encounter with Jesus. Some testimonies can be dramatic "Damascus road" type of experiences; but for most people it has been a gradual growth in faith with some significant moments of encounter. One type of experience is not better than the other. The main thing is that we are witnessing to how Jesus has made a difference in our lives. Because it is your story it is good to give sufficient detail to the way that Jesus has come into your life. It isn't advisable to spend too much time sharing about the darkness of sin committed in the past, but rather to focus on the change that has come because of Jesus.

When sharing about our lives as Christians it is important on the one hand to witness to the joy of our new life in the Lord; but on the other hand to be realistic about the ongoing struggle in our lives. We do not want to convey that being a Christian is just negative, boring, and full of painful self-denial. It needs to be a witness of fullness of life found in Jesus, and new power to overcome old habits. But we don't want to create an unreal expectancy of a perfect life just around the corner. Testimonies should in some way invite a response, whether it is just to keep the conversation going into the future, or maybe to read something or watch some video on YouTube, or, if the person seems open and ready, to ask whether you can pray with the person.

11
THE GIFT OF HEALING

If we are moving under the grace of the new Pentecost, the ministry of healing will be integral to our evangelising work. Healing is at the heart of the proclamation of the gospel.[98] Jesus sent them out "to proclaim the kingdom of God and to heal" (Lk 9:2). Spirit-filled preaching will always be accompanied by physical, emotional and spiritual healing. In our day this is more important than ever. In a secularised world God seems to be absent. People are spiritual orphans, feeling lost and abandoned. In this context, the manifestation of healing gifts can be a powerful means of convincing people of the incarnate presence of Christ.

The proclamation of the good news is not meant only to be words, but also to be accompanied by signs and wonders. Especially in a visual age when people want evidence of the veracity of what is preached, healing speaks loudly. In addition the current break down in family relationships, the increase of domestic violence and the general harshness of relating in the society means that many are the "walking wounded", bearing heavy interior burdens, struggling to keep their head above water. No wonder Pope Francis likens the Church to a field hospital in the midst of a battle. With people devastated from life circumstances, prostrate and critically wounded, words are not enough; they need to be accompanied by the power of healing. To proclaim the word of God without offering the healing of Jesus is to bring only half the message of salvation. As Pope Benedict XVI said,

"Christianity is a therapeutic religion"; healing, he explained, is "an essential dimension of our apostolic mission".[99]

Jesus Healed

In the gospels Jesus healed everyone who came to him. They merely had to reach out and touch the fringe of his cloak (Mk 6:56; Mt 13:46; Lk 6:18-19). He responded to people with great faith and to those who have little faith (Mk 1:40-41; 9:23; Mt 9:28-29). Sometimes he healed when there was no faith evident at all (Jn 5:7). His compassion knew no bounds. He wanted his disciples to share this ministry. When the 72 disciples, who had been sent out, returned and told of the healings and deliverance that happened when they pronounced his name, Jesus was elated. He rejoiced with a blessing prayer to the Father for revealing these things to little ones, while they are hidden from the wise and clever of this world (Lk 10: 21). Jesus promised that all who believe in him would "perform the same works as I do myself, they will perform even greater works, because I am going to the Father" (Jn 14:12).

All of Jesus' ministry was done in the power of the Holy Spirit. In the synagogue in Nazareth he quoted Isaiah, "The Spirit of the Lord is upon me. He has anointed me". Jesus wants us also to share in this anointing. The word Christian means, the "anointed one". In our sacramental and charismatic ministry we continue the healing mission of Jesus in the world today. Jesus commissioned us, "All authority in heaven and in earth has been given to me. Go therefore…" (Mt 28:18-20). We have the authority to act in his name. In the sacramental ministry of the Church the priest acts in the name of Jesus as Head of the Church. This is a particularly powerful apostolic authority which is guaranteed to be effective. But it would be a mistake to restrict healing ministry to the sacraments. All disciples have been commissioned to pray for, and to command, healing in the name of Jesus.

> Go out to the whole world; proclaim the good news to all creation. He who believes and is baptised will be saved; he who does not believe will be condemned. These are the signs that will be associated with believers: in my name they will cast out devils; they will have the gift of tongues....they will lay their hands on the sick, who will recover. (Mk 16:16-18)

As disciples of Jesus, sons and daughters of God, we move under the anointing of the Spirit and like the early apostles we can step out in faith and bring healing.

Apostolic Experience of Healing

After Pentecost the apostles were quick to move under the anointing given them. When Peter and John were on their way to the Temple for 3pm prayers Peter encountered a crippled man begging at the Beautiful Gate. Peter had nothing with which to help the man. They were carrying no money. But in the midst of the milling crowd he made an amazing act of faith. He said to the man, "I have neither silver nor gold, but I will give you what I have: in the name of Jesus Christ the Nazarene, walk" (Acts 3:6). He took hold of the man's hand and raised him up. The man, totally healed, went into the Temple with them "walking and jumping and praising God". With such a sensational demonstration of the Spirit, people gathered quickly to witness the miracle. Peter immediately took the opportunity to preach the *kerygma*. He simply proclaimed that this healing happened through the power which was released when the name of Jesus was pronounced in faith. It was not Peter who did it but Jesus (Acts 3:16).

This gift of healing given to the Twelve was soon flowing through other members of the Church. Stephen we are told "did great wonders and signs among the people" (Acts 6:8) before he was martyred. In Samaria Philip won many people to the faith in Christ through his powerful ministry: "For unclean spirits came out of many who were possessed, crying with a loud voice; and many who were paralysed or lame were healed" (Acts 8:7). As Paul and Barnabas preached in Iconium the Lord "bore witness to the word of his grace, granting signs and wonders to be done by their hands" (Acts 14:3). Paul's missionary work included curing a lame man, casting out a spirit from a possessed girl, raising a young man from the dead, and healing a man with dysentery. In Ephesus we are told, "God did extraordinary miracles by the hands of Paul, so that handkerchiefs or aprons were carried away from his body to the sick, and diseases left them and the evil spirits came out of them" (Acts 19:11-12).

Jesus sent them out to "proclaim that the kingdom of God is close at hand". In doing this he commissioned them to "cure the sick, raise the dead, cleanse the lepers, cast out devils" (Mt 10: 8-9). In other words they were to know the authority given to them, and act with that authority. No doubt they prayed to the Lord for his help, but the act of healing was done by an authoritative command in the name of Jesus. He had promised that after the resurrection they would be "clothed with power from on high" (Lk 24:49). They knew that "power" had been bestowed upon them. Jesus had promised, "you will receive power when the Holy Spirit comes upon you..." (Acts 1:8). Paul reminded the Corinthians that he did not come with words of great eloquence, but with "a demonstration of the *power* of the Spirit" (1Cor 2:4-5). The miracles that accompanied his proclamation proved that Jesus was indeed alive and at work in the world. They also convinced his hearers that what he proclaimed was the truth. This leaves a question begging for us to ponder. Do we prayerfully expect the manifest power of the Holy Spirit in our evangelising work?

Are we lacking in expectant faith, limiting the supernatural action of God, preferring the safety of relying on own plans and resources, and hence opting for a mediocre response?

History of Healing in the Church

The gift of supernatural healing was very much part of the evangelising work of the early Church. Justin Martyr (100-165 AD) testifies to what they were experiencing in Rome. He wrote to the unbelievers, giving them reason to believe:

> Jesus was born by the will of God the Father for the salvation of believers and the destruction of demons. And now you can learn this by what you see with your own eyes. For throughout the world and in your city there are many demoniacs whom all the other exorcists, sorcerers and magicians could not heal, but whom our Christians have healed and do heal, disabling and casting out the demons who possessed them in the name of Jesus Christ who was crucified under Pontius Pilate.[100]

Miracles happened through the ministry of ordinary Christians while spreading the gospel. Origen (184-253AD) shows that miracles done in the name of Jesus by the simplest of people are a powerful witness. Christians cast out demons, he said:

> without the use of any curious arts of magic, or incantations, but merely by prayer and simple adjurations which the plainest person can use. Because for the most part it is uneducated persons who perform this work, thus making manifest the grace that is the word of Christ and the despicable weakness of demons.[101]

When the unbelievers saw sick people totally healed in the name of Jesus they saw the good news before their very eyes. They found a new hope that they could be set free from darkness and come to the light of Christ. All that held them captive could be overcome. The signs and wonders accompanying the proclamation of the gospel won the people to embrace this whole new way of life in Christ.

St Augustine (354-430) originally did not expect the charism of healing to be operative in his day. But in his *Retractions*, written towards the end of his life, Augustine admitted he was wrong in denying healing.[102] He had actually seen with his own eyes major healings happening in his liturgical assemblies and was convinced that the Lord still did miracles in the present. In fact he began to record the many miracles in the Church at Hippo. He says:

> I realised how many miracles were occurring in our own day… which were like the miracles of old, and how wrong it would be to allow the memory of these miracles of divine power to perish among the people…It is only two years ago that the keeping of records was begun here in Hippo, and already, at this writing, we have more than seventy attested miracles.[103]

With the experience of the new Pentecost today across all the Christian Churches we are seeing a new manifestation of charisms, including that of healing and deliverance. Healing Masses and rallies are now commonplace and the healing gifts have become integral to the work of evangelisation.

Praying for Physical Healing

In the work of the new evangelisation we can expect physical healings to occur when the word is proclaimed. How can we dispose ourselves to allow the Holy Spirit to work more powerfully through us in this way? We need to know more fully who we really are in God and act accordingly. We have to believe what he says about us and what he has commissioned us to do. We call this "moving under the anointing of the Spirit". This means stepping out in faith, taking a risk, and putting everything in the hands of the Lord. It also means expecting great things of the Lord. Jesus told us to "Ask and you will receive, seek and you will find, knock and the door will be opened to you..." (Lk 11:9). He also said, "Have faith in God. I tell you solemnly, if anyone says to this mountain, 'Get up and throw yourself into the sea', with no hesitation in his heart but believing that what he says will happen, it will be done for him. I tell you therefore: everything you ask and pray for, believe that you have it already, and it will be yours" (Mk 11: 23-24). The problem is not that we ask too much of God, but that we ask too little. God is not limited in any way, and he is not sparing in his gifts. We do not receive because we do not expect enough, and do not ask for enough.

When praying for healing it is important to listen attentively to the direction of the Lord. As Mary said at Cana to the servants, "Do whatever he tells you" (Jn 2:5). As a result of simple obedience, doing something that made no sense at all, namely filling large jars with water, they were rewarded. This is how water is changed into wine; by obedience. Listening to the Lord, you may receive a prophetic word for the person which is a key to unlock something, which opens the way for healing. Or the Lord may give you a "word of knowledge" which can communicate clearly to the person what the Lord wants to heal, and so inspire their faith to receive the healing. Words of knowledge are not meant to create curiosity, but to build faith in the person, who opens up to the healing that Jesus wants to bring. When praying with someone, or when absorbed in communal worship, a person with this prophetic gifting will have a sense that the Lord is wanting to do a specific healing and will communicate this. When the word is given it arouses faith in the person for healing, and Jesus brings the healing as promised.

Miracles Do Happen

Often the word of knowledge simply announces what the Lord is already doing, regardless of the faith of the one being healed. Last year, Lalith Perera, a Catholic lay evangelist in Sri Lanka, and his team were invited to conduct a parish Lenten retreat program. Disappointingly for the organisers only 15 people turned up for the first night. The organisers were apologetic, but the team were eager to go ahead anyway. After the preaching there was a time of charismatic praise before the Blessed Sacrament. During praise time Lalith sensed strongly that someone present had a crooked leg and that the Lord wanted to heal it. Giving this word seemed risky since the odds of this specific problem being present in such a small group were very short indeed. When he announced the word of knowledge no one responded. Later during the prayer meeting he was so convinced of the word that he brought it to the group again. Still no response, and they left for home wondering whether it may have been a mistake.

The next day Lalith received an excited phone call from the parish. A woman who had attended the Lenten program had begged her daughter to come with her. The daughter, who was 19 years old, had suffered a serious car accident months earlier. As a result her leg had been twisted up around her neck. After intensive surgery, with the help of steel pins, doctors were able to straighten her leg somewhat and had promised she would be able to walk. But she had not been able to do so, and was bitter about the crippled state of her crooked leg. The mother had been keen that her daughter would come to the retreat since she knew there would be prayers for healing. However, the young woman had refused, telling her mother that she had given up on God. After praying for his help her prayers had not been answered.

When the mother returned home from the retreat she said to her daughter. "You should have come. There was a word given that was just for you." The girl was taken aback and asked quietly, "What time was the word given?" The mother told her it was at 1.00pm. The daughter became very excited. She told her mother that she had been sleeping during the morning and at lunch-time, which was at 1.00pm, she had got up and walked to the table. It was only after lunch, as she began to return to her bedroom, she realised that she was actually walking! She showed her mother, "Look, I can walk! And what about this, I can run!" When the young woman shared her testimony of healing at the local community, they asked her to show them how she could run. She said, "I can do more. Look, I can dance!" In a mysterious way God wants to involve us in his healing work. We need to be listening for the liberating word which can set another free.

A Culture of Testimony

A key factor for any Christian community, whether it be a parish, or a new ecclesial community, is that it fosters a culture of testimony. When healings happen they should not be kept secret. We have a responsibility to let the light of Jesus shine; this increases faith in everyone. Testimonies are stories of God's intervention in our lives. They should be preserved, kept honest and discussed in conversations. Any time we share about the marvellous works of God we give him glory and we build up the environment of faith in the community. Testimonies don't only help us to remember past actions of God; they also reveal what God wants to do now. They stir up expectant faith for God's healing to take place again in our midst. People who are timid in their attempts to witness to Jesus become bold disciples after seeing the Lord's miraculous action. By recording what God has done in the past, similar to what St Augustine did, this provides a lens through which to see present situations. We believe more strongly that we have a God of the impossible. Every time we share a testimony with someone of the marvellous works of God we give our listeners an opportunity to taste of the mercy of God.

Sacraments of Healing

The Church's primary way of praying for the sick is by the sacraments of healing – the Anointing of the Sick, Reconciliation and the Eucharist. James says, "If anyone is sick, he should send for the elders of the church, and they must anoint him with oil in the name of the Lord and pray over him. The prayer of faith will save the sick man and the Lord will raise him up again" (James 5:14-15). Prior to Vatican II this sacrament was focussed on preparing the person for death, but now it is restored to being the sacrament for the sick, whereby the Church prays for healing of body, mind and spirit. We cannot underestimate its power. Physical healings often happen when this sacrament is ministered in faith. The regular celebration of the sacrament in a communal context provides a rich opportunity for evangelisation.

The Sacrament of Reconciliation brings the deepest healing through forgiveness of sins. But it also can become a means of healing of hurts that aren't immediately obvious to the penitent. Underlying the sin confessed there can be deeper wounds associated with the sin. In the context of a relaxed face to face encounter with the priest penitents can talk about the deeper dilemmas of their lives, and be helped to make decisions necessary for growth in the Lord's ways. Often the presenting sin is only the tip of the iceberg. Underneath there is a whole complexity of wounds that need healing. Without labouring the issue the priest can help the penitent turn their wounds towards Jesus, for his gentle, healing touch. In addition there is a long tradition in the Church of minor exorcism, or deliverance, ministered in the sacrament. The priest may sense some demonic bondage which needs a prayer of authority to release the person. He may discuss this with the person in a way that is not frightening for them, or in some cases he may simply command the demon to loosen its hold on the penitent under his breath.

The Sacrament of the Eucharist is powerful for healing. Often people will experience a whole new sense of peace and hope after receiving Jesus in communion. Sometimes physical healings happen as well. After all, the same Jesus who walked the laneways of Galilee and never refused anyone a healing is just as really present to us in the Eucharist. Just as the woman who had the haemorrhage for twelve years reached out in desperation to touch the hem of his cloak, we also can reach out to touch him in Eucharist.[104]

Need for Inner Healing

The new evangelisation touches into the deepest areas of brokenness in people's lives. Inner healing prayer addresses the interior wounds and agonising memories of the past. The message of God's love opens up the pain that people can be suffering – abandonment, loss, loneliness, anxiety, anger, fear, guilt, shame and a whole range of emotions. The healing prayer invites Jesus into these traumatic events of the past. Jesus comes to take the poison out of the wound, so it can be remembered in a new light. Often the minister will invite the person firstly to get in touch with the depth of the pain and not to deny the truth of its effect upon them. Also, through gentle prayer, the Holy Spirit may reveal the root causes of the negative memory from years ago. Then the person may need to forgive those who were responsible for the affliction, and may need to ask the Lord for forgiveness for holding resentment against those responsible. Here the sacrament of Reconciliation may be appropriate. They then may be invited to imagine Jesus coming into the painful memory and allow Jesus to bring healing, and a new sense of security, peace and new life.

We have discovered that interior psychic pain is often manifest in physical ailments.[105] The presenting physical illness is a sign of some deeper emotional anguish or disorder. Some would say that as much as 80% of sicknesses have some psychosomatic dimension. For example, repressed anxiety, nervous tension, guilt, anger, can manifest in physical symptoms. In addition there are many well-known stress related conditions such as ulcers, heart abnormalities, skin eruptions etc. The presenting problem is but the tip of the iceberg which is mainly hidden underneath the surface and needs to be melted by the experience of God's healing love. Here it is important to understand that all healing of Jesus is not just a manifestation of his power, but even more so an expression of his abounding compassion and love. We do not rely on any particular technique or formula or any particular process. Healing is a work of the Spirit of love. It is his love that touches hearts, minds and bodies. In the healing ministry the most important quality we need to have is the loving heart of Jesus who lives within us. There are no infallible techniques that work. It is only love.

Praying for Inner Healing

When ministering healing we are not to be too overbearing or intimidating. We are simply wounded healers. We minister with a compassionate heart, trusting that Jesus will bring about what is needed. Without being intrusive, and with permission, we can use touch as a way of establishing human connection, a gesture of solidarity, warmth and reassurance e.g. a hand on the shoulder. When praying we focus on the love of God and help people look beyond their suffering to Jesus; to raise their hearts and minds to the God of all love. The prayer should not be too complicated, but simple and related to the pain in the heart. It is good sometimes to imaginatively visualise what is happening, and lead the person to picture Jesus beside the person, reaching out his hand and touching the person's affliction. We always finish with a time of thanking and praising God for his goodness, and expressing our confidence that he is doing what we have requested. While the healing prayer has opened the hurts of the past that have been buried, and may give rise to strong emotions, we do not want to leave people in their vulnerability, but to centre everything in Christ. We are there to point them to Jesus, to help them encounter the healing of Jesus, who relieves the pain and brings his peace.

A further point needs to be made. A major obstacle to inner healing is refusal to forgive.[106] Buried resentment twists up the spirit of a person and literally paralyses them, making it impossible to be healed. People trapped in this vengeful mentality hold up a fist inside themselves against someone or some group who has hurt them, and their inner rage can often manifest in physical sickness such as arthritis. They need to let go of the judgements against the other and give the judgement over to God. They must make a decision to forgive, regardless of the emotions. The feelings can catch up later, but under God's grace we can always decide to forgive. To forgive is not to condone the offense, nor is it to excuse the offender. Genuine forgiveness is only made when in the light of my clear understanding that a grave injustice has been made to me, and allowing myself to feel its pain completely, I still choose to let it go inside myself. This decision under God's grace is the greatest thing a human being can do and it sets us free interiorly making it possible for our healing to take place.

There is a beautiful mutual reinforcement of love between the moment of preaching and the moment of healing. Often in today's world people who are suffering from traumas of the past, or struggling with close relationships, or grief-stricken due to loss of a loved one, or despairing over a son or a daughter, are not open to hearing the word preached. They feel incapable of change. They often carry undue levels of shame and guilt, and feel dragged down into a depressive vortex. They simply need compassion and love. They need someone to listen to them unconditionally. They need to unburden their mess without any judgement laid upon them. This is where the healing ministry is needed even before the preaching. On the other hand, if the preaching is truly proclaiming the love of God and touching into the deepest cries of the heart it can arouse in a person the desire for healing. They realise that the sinful areas of their life, maybe addictive patterns, have deeper roots that can only be dealt with through prayer for inner healing. Consequently, often on weekends, retreats and conferences, after the sacrament of Reconciliation we may have some time for inner healing prayer before the Blessed Sacrament, helping participants to bring their wounded selves to the Lord, just as they are and, like the adulterous woman in the gospel, experience his unconditional acceptance and love.

Activity of Evil Spirits

Jesus spent time casting out demons, and he gave us authority to cast them out in his name. When the 72 disciples returned after their mission they exultantly reported to Jesus, "even the demons submit to us when we use your name" (Lk 10:17). Jesus agreed that he had given them power to conquer the whole strength of the enemy, but warned them not to take any pride in that. Rather to keep in their minds and rejoice "that your names are written in the book of life". In other words we need to accept the authority given us, but not let it go to our heads!

When it comes to dealing with evil spirits there are two extremes.

The first, which is unfortunately quite common in the Church, is to disbelieve in their existence and explain away the multitude of gospel texts by some "demythologising" theory, suggesting Jesus was just dealing with psychological problems. The purported activity of the Devil is derived from an overwrought mediaeval imagination. The second extreme is to cultivate an unhealthy or even obsessive interest in evil spirits, becoming over-spiritualised, expecting a demon to be found under every bush. We do not do the mission of Jesus in today's world any good with either of these extreme attitudes.

Lucifer and his fallen angels operate in this world for the destruction of human beings. They hate God and everything of God. Since they cannot harm God, they seek to harm human beings who are created in the image and likeness of God. Satan is the enemy of our human nature and we would be foolish to ignore this reality. However, the victory over Satan has already been won by Christ through his death and resurrection. Satan knows he is a defeated foe, but if we give him an opening he will furiously seek to destroy us. He is called in scripture "a liar from the beginning", a "murderer", "the accuser of the brethren", "the thief who comes to steal, kill and destroy". If we remain in Christ we need have no fear of evil spirits. Paul encourages us to be strong in the spiritual battle by putting on God's armour (Eph 6:10-17).

The enemy attacks us often by temptations. This calls for daily vigilance. However, the activity of evil spirits can be damaging in other ways as well. When we evangelise, Satan's strongholds are being routed. He is absolutely furious about this, and will fling against our efforts whatever opposition he can muster. Computers may mysteriously dysfunction, accidents occur, confusion in messages, and other incidents that could possibly be explained by natural causes. But often the unusual confluence of these disruptions indicates they are stirred up by evil spirits. The Catholic principle is to evaluate by always looking at natural causes first and only when things are unexplainable should we investigate the possibility of supernatural causes. While we cannot always be sure, we have definitely found that soaking our evangelistic outreaches in intercessory prayer makes for smooth running of events and protects against any demonic interference.

Another way the evil spirits operate is by seeking entry into the lives of vulnerable people who may have unwittingly opened a door giving them access. A classic case is someone who has become involved in the occult e.g. fortune telling, tarot cards, ouija boards, psychic healing, magic, witchcraft, etc. This is Satan's territory, and if we enter it we are asking for trouble. Some people go so far as to make self-inflicted curses or pacts with the devil. They definitely need deliverance. Some give access to evil spirits by obsessive sin, such as sexual addiction, pornography, compulsive lying or thieving. This bondage to perverse besetting sin can provide entry. Sometimes even a deep trauma kept in the darkness can be latched onto by an evil spirit. In each case the ministry of deliverance is simply a way of helping the person close the door on the evil spirit which has had easy access to come to disturb and partially control that area of a person's life.

Praying for Deliverance

The prayer for deliverance is best done within the wider context of inner healing prayer.[107] It is simply one dimension of this way of praying in order to free the person to claim who he or she is as a son or daughter of God. The steps are a way of evangelising the person; helping them to meet Jesus, the Saviour, who will deliver them from their bondage. From the outset it is important that the person expresses his or her faith in Jesus as their Saviour and Lord, even if their faith may still be weak and confused.[108] They need to identify any sinful areas in their personal story, confess the sin honestly, and turn to Jesus. Deliverance breaks the power behind habitual patterns of thinking and acting that limit freedom to accept the love of God and turn away from whatever blocks that love. The person is encouraged to take responsibility for his or her life and expose the lies by which they may have been living.

For freedom it is important for the person to forgive whoever has offended them or hurt them in any way. Forgiveness as we have seen is a decision. They have to overcome the desire for revenge and retaliation; to withdraw judgements and give it all to God. Once genuine forgiveness has been given the person needs to renounce what has been uncovered as the lies that they have owned. They need to declare that they want no more to do with these lies or empty promises, e.g. they identify a lie of rejection, name it for what it is, and renounce it. Renouncing in the name of Jesus means that the person is claiming through the power of Jesus that this thing will have no more influence on their life. It is a choice not to be a victim anymore; a choice to take responsibility. For example an abuse victim can be lost in a maze of shame, blame, anger, a sense of helplessness. They can now stand up and be who they are; a son or daughter of God, saved by the precious blood of Jesus.

At this point the one who is the minister of deliverance simply makes an authoritative command in the name of Jesus that the power of every evil spirit that has been renounced will now leave this person. This is not spoken in one's own authority, but through the authority of Jesus. It is Jesus bringing about the kingdom, not us. Then finally we call on the Father to pour out his blessing. This is the time for the person to be filled again with the healing love of God. It is time to claim again one's true identity in God. This sort of deliverance prayer does not have to be dramatic with exotic manifestations. Once the door has been closed on evil spirits as long as the person keeps up a strong spiritual life with regular Eucharist, daily prayer, reading the word of God, committing to discipleship within a Christian community, they need have no fear of evil spirits bothering them again.

12
A COMMUNITY OF DISCIPLES ON MISSION

Most practising Catholics unfortunately still have a sadly deficient experience of Church. The parish Sunday Mass is often a gathering of isolated and anonymous individuals praying together but rarely connecting in any meaningful way with one another. One of our biggest challenges is to develop real, face to face, Christian community. Many parishioners drive into the parish Church for Sunday Eucharist and rush out again after the dismissal with minimal contact with others. I once heard it cynically likened to using the Church like a drive in-drive out "fast food" outlet, or like a quick spiritual fill-up at the petrol station. We all sense this is inadequate and are hungry for ways to overcome the problem. An authentic community is a place where each person is known and loved. It's a place where we share one another's burdens and care for one another in a real and practical way. This question of how to build genuine community is crucial for the new evangelisation. We do not evangelise as individuals, but as Church. The whole community needs to be on a missionary footing. And when we reach out to people, and they respond, where can we bring them? Where can we find a vibrant, welcoming community? If this reality does not exist, all our individual efforts to evangelise are in vain.

Welcomed and Belonging
The drift of people from the Catholic Church to evangelical or Pente-

costal groups may have many reasons. But it is rarely due to a protest about beliefs. Usually it is because they found a sense of belonging, felt welcomed, and found a more personal faith in Jesus. The present generation are not so much seeking a comprehensive belief system, but are hungry for relationship. In the context of a warm, friendly, compassionate community they are more likely to open up to the faith in a new way and live the life of a disciple of Christ.[109] This is a reversal of what we would naturally think. From my theological training I would expect that good spiritual homilies and teachings, as well as provision of opportunities to take up programs of renewal, would be sufficient to get the change required in people to conform their beliefs and behaviours to the way of Jesus and his Church. But only 10% of the people in the pews on Sunday are likely to take up these opportunities for spiritual growth. The rest remain unchanged. While this has implications for retention of membership in the Church, it also has implications for our mission to the alienated and unchurched.

What attracts post-modern people to a community first is not the belief system but the warmth of welcome. Pope Francis says that the evangeliser must have "certain attitudes which foster openness to the message: approachability, readiness to dialogue, patience, a warmth and welcome that is non-judgemental."[110] We need to reach out to the one who is not yet ready to believe, and not yet ready to take on our Christian way of life. We need to love that person into the kingdom of God, and into the Church, and eventually into a journey of discipleship within the Church. If they feel loved, and feel they truly belong, they gradually will be open to accepting beliefs, and especially as they come into living relationship with Jesus they will begin to want to change their disordered behaviour. Pope Francis says, "The Church must be a place of mercy freely given, where everyone can feel welcomed, loved, forgiven and encouraged to live the good life of the gospel."¹¹¹ The challenge is to build a culture where there is a warm, welcoming, non-judgemental environment in which people do not feel threatened or pressured into anything.

Focussed Outwards

The evangelising community will always be looking beyond itself. It will not have the "private club" mentality, as if it existed for its own members. Rather it will be going out to the fringes to encounter the marginalised, seeking those who have fallen away, or those who have never had contact with Christianity before. They will stand at the crossroads and welcome the outcast. They will be rich in mercy and will be ready to wash the feet of others in imitation of Jesus, the Master. It is a community where people's daily lives matter, where all their pain and struggles of life are born together. It is a supportive community, standing by people at every step of their journey. It is a community which is patient with others and their many failings, ready to help them in their time of distress. But it is not turned inward upon itself, but always going forth, since it exists to welcome the stranger. As Pope Francis has repeated often, the Church is for everyone, beginning with the marginalised. This means that we need a special eye for the visitor, the one who may be turning up for family reasons, or may just happen to arrive randomly. No one should feel left out or ignored; all are desired by the heart of Jesus.

A New Home

David and Teresa were political refugees from El Salvador living in Canberra. It had been hard leaving the familiarity of home and coming to a strange new country. They were low in spirits, lonely and homesick. They were questioning whether they had made the right decision, leaving their family and homeland, even though they were grateful to be safe from danger. David had a Baptist background and was feeling the need for spiritual support. He had been browsing the newspapers looking for a church. Teresa was a Catholic but was no longer practising her faith. She too was feeling an ache for more. After visiting the Civic Library, they were walking to the bus through Garema Place, when they were approached by a married couple carrying a Bible. They did not feel affronted, but rather glad that someone wanted to talk with them. They said afterwards that they were really spiritually hungry, but had not clearly identified this. Now, after an initial chat with this friendly couple they were very open when the couple asked if they wanted to know Jesus. They said "yes", and so the couple prayed with them. The prayer was not long, but it felt like gentle rain on their souls. David asked the couple, "Where do you worship?" They said, "We are Catholics". He was very surprised, since he had no idea that Catholics would do that sort of thing.

After meeting other members of the team, David and Teresa gladly accepted an invitation to come to a Catholic community gathering the next Sunday. A member of the community offered them a lift. They felt so welcome and in the worship songs they felt the presence of God. Teresa said, "I felt God was welcoming me through these people. I just felt they were looking upon me with God's mercy, love and trust". Growing up in a country where they felt they could not trust anyone, they were deeply touched. They felt trusted by people who had just met them. They were invited to have dinner with a family the next day. Teresa said, "Without knowing us they trusted us; it was God's welcome". That same evening they attended a charismatic Mass together and decided that the Catholic Church was their home. David entered into full communion with the Church and Teresa reclaimed her faith as well. Now they have long-standing friends in the Church and remain dedicated followers of the Lord.

From Maintenance to Mission

Pope Francis warns that new programs alone are not what we need. In his document, *The Joy of the Gospel*, he makes his "I have a dream!" statement. Today's situation calls for a whole new paradigm: "I have a dream of a 'missionary option', that is, a missionary impulse capable of transforming everything."[112] He calls us out of "ecclesial introversion" to be thoroughly mission-oriented. Our customs, ways of doing things, schedules, language and structures all need to be focussed on evangelisation. As a Church we need to move from preoccupation with maintenance to a passion for mission. He says, "We cannot passively and calmly wait in our Church buildings"; we must be constantly going forth with joyful proclamation.[113] Quoting the *Aparecida* document he calls for a Church which is "permanently in a state of mission".[114] At Rio de Janeiro World Youth day he said to the young people, "I want you to make yourselves heard...I want the noise to go out. I want the Church to go out onto the streets"; he is calling for a Church that intentionally moves from self-preservation to mission. He tells us that the most disturbing reality for the Church is "the fact that so many of our brothers and sisters are living without the strength, light and consolation born of friendship with Jesus Christ, without a community of faith to support them, without meaning and a goal in life".[115]

Within the hostile environment of today's Western culture the temptation could be to engage in a sort of "strategic withdrawal" into sheltered communities.[116] In order to withstand the storm we could bunch together against the prevailing darkness and keep the light burning amongst ourselves until the new dawn arrives. We could simply wait out this generation's "barbaric" tendencies in a ghetto and pray for a change to come in the future. This is a popular thesis presented today, but it is flawed, simply because we don't exist to preserve ourselves. We exist as a community to evangelise. This is not a time to become defensive and inward looking. Our whole purpose is to build a new civilisation of life and love "brick by brick", as Pope John Paul II urged the young people at World Youth Day in Canada.[117] Our intentional Christian communities will hopefully shed the light of Christ in the darkness and show the way to live through our witness of life. But we will not be turned in upon ourselves. Rather we will be aiming to influence the hostile culture and find ways to help change it. The game is not up. We have only just begun to engage the modern world with the gospel. There are many hopeful signs that people today out of sheer frustration with the secularist experiment are opening up to the gospel message. It is not a time to be on the back foot, but to be firmly on the front foot seeking new and creative opportunities to win people to Christ.

A Christian Culture

While we must be outward focussed, at the same time our communities need to develop a distinctive Christian culture vis-a-vis the modern secular, individualistic mind-set of our times. The issue of culture is vital. So much of the world around us is incompatible with the gospel. This makes community life critically important. Children need to learn to be non-conformist with many of the current values and attitudes in the society; families need to be strengthened and held together in prayer and holiness; parishes need to become communities of communities so that all parishioners can belong to a face to face group with whom they share life and love. New ecclesial communities need to serve the whole Church for its renewal rather than isolate themselves with their own agendas.

The actual culture of any community often remains hidden and unnamed. In schools we call it the "hidden curriculum". Culture is the common way of life, the common understanding of life, and the common set of values. It expresses how the community defines itself and how it envisages its role in the world.[118] It is often subliminal, yet with significant formative power. The culture of a community shapes its members more than any intentional effort of preaching or instruction. Much of community renewal involves identifying the operative culture and changing it to express what we really want to achieve. James Mallon says, "I am convinced the primary challenge of the new evangelisation is nothing short of the transformation of the cultures of our churches, which means a conversion of values."[119] Culture speaks of what is really happening rather than what theory we have about it. We don't need to change our doctrines or moral teaching, but we do need to get in touch with the real values that are being imparted to people of all different ages and stages in our communities. This "hidden curriculum" can hold us back from going forward in evangelisation.

The leaders of a parish or diocese may decide on a new strategy for change and throw endless resources into making it work, but if the culture of the members is a stoic attitude of business as usual, expecting little more than the quiet satisfaction that religious chores have been fulfilled, the grand strategy will inevitably fail. As the old saying goes, "culture will eat strategy for breakfast".[120] Even more so if the culture of the members is in continuum with the worldly values of their contemporaries, the strategy for renewal will not have a chance. We need a transformation of Church culture which happens from the inside to the outside, by genuine personal conversion under the power of the Spirit and development of communities of disciples that carry the values of the Kingdom of God.

Making Disciples

I would maintain that every Catholic needs to be part of a small faith community which is supportive and challenging in their Christian life. This is the way of discipleship. Jesus said, "Go, make disciples" (Mt 28:19). He did not only commission us to make sure everyone belongs to a parish congregation. Nor did he only commission us to ensure everyone opens their heart to the word and welcomes his saving love, as important as this is. He commissioned us to "make disciples". Any Catholic community must have this agenda. For this to happen we must drop the clericalised model of Church where the priest is expected to do all the spiritual work and the lay people help out here and there with practical administration. The new ecclesial communities which are led and pastored by lay people witness to the power of the laity in evangelising and making disciples. Many parishes are beginning to catch on to this as well. Within the context of small communities people who are seeking to grow in the way of Jesus can get the help they need and be accompanied on the journey of discipleship.

Accompaniment

Pope Francis appeals to all in the Church to grow in the "art of accompaniment".[121] This privilege of accompanying another on their journey of faith can happen most effectively in the context of a closely related Christian community. By accompaniment he means walking with the other in a caring, non-judgmental companionship in order to lead them into a closer relationship with the Lord. He encourages those who accompany others to develop good listening skills. Only by listening closely to the other will we find the true way to encourage them in the way God is calling them. It requires prudence, patience, discernment and docility to the Holy Spirit. Only by respectful and compassionate listening can we help the other to grow in their desire for Christ and be strengthened in their way of being his disciple. Growing to maturity in Christ takes time, and often involves some failures along the way. The one accompanying needs to stay with their friend through thick and thin, realising that attaining maturity of faith calls for much time and patience. Any community should be seeking to empower missionary disciples to accompany others into becoming missionary disciples as well.

Relationship Evangelisation

Relationship is the key to personal evangelisation. A natural relationship through family, work, or student environment can develop without any manipulation into a way of accompaniment. We don't see the other as a "potential recruit", but as a unique individual loved by God. The initial relationship is simply friendly, not business-like; maybe meeting for coffee, inviting home for a meal. Listening to the other shows you respect them and affirms the person in their talents and passion. Listening also helps to discover where the person's deepest needs are. In these settings God-given moments arise when questions are asked and it is simple to share who you are and the relationship you have discovered with the Lord. We do well to avoid any religious jargon, but simply to share respectfully and tactfully what is the love of your life. Just share who Jesus is to you in a simple and relevant way. Then inviting the person to the community of faith opens the opportunity for them to hear the gospel preached and to make a response. Gradually they become at home and want to continue with the community.

When someone has opened their life to Jesus as the loving Saviour and Lord, and asked for the new outpouring of the Holy Spirit, we need to accompany them towards maturity in Christ. You don't have to be perfect to do this. You are not relating as a saint to a sinner; rather like one beggar showing another where to find the bread. When you walk with a new disciple it is important to be open and vulnerable yourself, inviting them to journey with you into a deeper place with God. Most importantly we need to encourage them, especially when they experience failure. We don't play God, but allow them to make mistakes, and be patient and never give up on them. Always point them towards Jesus, and avoid taking personal responsibility for their decisions. You are a listening ear; not the one who makes their decisions. Often pray for the person, and seek the Lord's heart for them. Needless to say this work of "making disciples" is very time consuming. Such a big investment is a slow, hard labour of love. There are many disappointments as some fall away, but there is great joy in nurturing the life of God in another, watching them grow.

It is important to avoid being the exclusive spiritual companion for the person. A good companion will want them to have access to a priest for the sacrament of reconciliation, and at the right time to find a competent spiritual director as well. In addition they will need to become integrated into the life of the community so it is really the whole body which incorporates them into Christ. They will especially need to feed on the Eucharist regularly, read the Scriptural word regularly, get into the habit of spiritual reading or listening to talks on videos or podcast, and attend some formation courses in the spiritual and moral life. Also from the moment they fall in love with Jesus and have a longing for him they need to develop a strong prayer life and become evangelists themselves. It is never too early for someone to begin sharing the love they have discovered in Jesus. All disciples are meant to evangelise even though they may be fresh in their initial encounter with Jesus. Testimonies of the recently converted are often the most powerful. They have a strong ring of credibility about them since the person tells the story without the benefit of a learned faith language. It powerfully speaks of the reality of Christ.

The Fruit of Disciples

The presence of a significant number of genuine disciples of Jesus in a community changes everything. The culture begins to change. The expectations in the community change; the whole spiritual tone lifts. There is a new energy level and a new hunger for God. As Sherry Weddel explains:

> Disciples pray with passion. Disciples worship. Disciples love the Church and serve her with energy and joy. Disciples give lavishly. Disciples hunger to learn more about their faith. Disciples fill every formation class in a parish or a diocese. Disciples manifest charisms and discern vocations. They clamour to discern God's call because they long to live it. Disciples evangelise because they have really good news to share. Disciples share their faith with their children. Disciples care about the poor and about issues of justice. Disciples take risks for the kingdom of God.[122]

The new evangelisation must have as its aim to "make disciples" as Jesus did. He modelled to us the strategy for evangelisation. Often he preached to the crowds and we also will find ourselves doing the same in large gatherings or rallies. But he spent time forming the 72 disciples and sent them out for training in evangelisation. This was closer and more intense work. Often in the gospels we see Jesus turn from the crowds and speak exclusively to the disciples. A disciple was one who had responded to the call to come out from the crowd; no longer following Jesus out of curiosity or expectation of signs and wonders. The disciple was to walk behind the Master, listen to his instruction and obey his call upon them. The disciple was to share in Jesus' journey to the cross: "Anyone who wants to be a follower of mine must take up his cross daily". Whatever was done to the Master would also be done to the disciple.

Then within this circle of disciples Jesus selected twelve who were to "be with him and be sent out to preach and deliver" (Mk 3:14). These he spent most of his time with. He lived with them, shared life together. He encouraged them, corrected them, listened, guided and imparted wisdom to them. Most of his energy went into forming them. Then even within the twelve he invited three, Peter, James and John, to the most profound moments of the Transfiguration and the Garden in Gethsemane. The temptation is to think we are wasting our time by having it consumed by forming disciples. But there is no more fruitful work for the kingdom.

If you focus on making disciples you multiply your effectiveness. Just imagine that a Catholic community of 100 true disciples decided that each member would be dedicated to make one more genuine disciple each year. If they all fulfilled their commitment, there would be 200 disciples at the end of the first year. If each of those new disciples also decided to make one disciple each year, and kept their commitment, then at the end of the next year there would be 400 disciples. If this principle was maintained faithfully, namely that every new disciple committed to simply make one more disciple each year, after 20 years the whole of Australia would be converted, even taking into account the expected population increase! Do the mathematics! This is the Lord's plan for evangelising the world.

13
PRIORITY OF THE POOR

Communities moving in the spirit of the new evangelisation will have an open door for everyone and be particularly concerned for those who are on the fringes of the society.

Pope Francis declared:

> If the whole Church takes up this missionary impulse, she has to go forth to everyone without exception. But to whom should she go first? When we read the gospel we find a clear indication: not so much our friends and wealthy neighbours, but above all the poor and the sick, those who are usually despised and overlooked, 'those who cannot repay you'.[123]

The missionary impulse will impel us to go beyond the comfort of our usual way of life and become aware of the poor. The greatest sin committed against the poor is indifference, pretending not to see. Like the priest and the Levite in the story of the Good Samaritan we can "pass by on the other side" (Lk 10:32). We can be blind to the plight of others and refuse to hear the cry of the poor. Like the rich man who feasted sumptuously every day we can be hard-hearted and ignore the man lying at the gate, covered with sores and longing for the scraps that fell from the rich man's table. Pope Francis suggests we can live behind "double glazing" which conveniently shuts out the cry of the poor. He warns against shutting ourselves up "within structures which give us a false sense of security, within rules which make us harsh judges, within habits which make us feel safe, while at the door people are starving". He says, "Jesus does not tire of saying to us: 'Give them something to eat".[124]

Aware of the Poor

The first challenge then is to *become aware* of the poor, who are closer than we think. We see them on our screens or in missionary magazines, but we are unaffected. We hear the Church's call to meet the poor, but we let it run past us. We have to break through the double glazing, overcome our indifference and insensitivity. We need a new depth of conversion of heart, which happens in the moment of encounter with the poor. We see this in the life of Francis of Assisi. As a well-heeled young man he naturally found lepers repulsive. But there came a grace-filled moment when he encountered a leper on the road coming towards him. Restraining his instinctive desire to run, Francis approached the leper and kissed him. Having already encountered the love of God in his heart, Francis now was experiencing in a real way the presence of Christ in the poor. A grace of practical love for the poor was born in him. We need a similar grace.

Jesus identified himself with the poor, the vulnerable and suffering. When speaking about those who did or did not care for the hungry, the thirsty, the stranger, the naked, the sick and those in prison he said "as often as you did it to the least of my brethren you did it to me" (Mt 25:40). He spoke of the poor with the same words he said at the Last Supper, "This is my body". When we meet the poor we touch the suffering body of Christ. Mother Teresa once told a story of a young sister who was struggling to find Jesus in the poor. She told the sister to watch carefully how tenderly the priest holds the consecrated host in the Mass, and then do the same while she is washing the sores of the people she was nursing that day. After a day of ministering within the house for the dying the young sister returned home delighted. She had recognised Jesus in the "distressing disguise of the poor". We find Christ not only in the poor who are members of the Church, but also in the poor of the world. All belong to the body of Christ. The words of Jesus make this clear, "As often as you did it to the least of my little ones, you did it to me" (Mt 25:40). This is not just a nice idea, but a reality. As a community of Christ we welcome all the poor as our own family, not in any way as alien or second rate. They are our true brothers and sisters in Christ.

Friendship With the Poor

The first movement to the poor is to establish relationship. We don't come in a superior way condescendingly giving "hand-outs" to salve our consciences. Rather we come to be in communion with our brothers and sisters in Christ. Even though they may not be baptised, Jesus has made them our brothers and sisters. In saying "blessed are you poor" Jesus "assured those burdened by sorrow and crushed by poverty that God has a special place for them in his heart".[125] We are a Church of the poor and for the poor. This is the heart of the Church's mission based on our faith in Christ. Our solidarity with the poor means that we respect the dignity of each person, and appreciate their goodness, their life-experience, and their ways of doing things. We come not only to bring something, but first of all to seek friendship, which will be a mutual giving and receiving. Pope Francis calls it "loving attentiveness", a true concern for the good of the other and to seek together with them what is best for them. We are called to be their friends, listen to them, and when necessary advocate for them. The key is a relationship that is mutually upbuilding. We come away from the encounter feeling we have received more than we have given. Pope Francis says:

> We need to let ourselves be evangelised by them. The new

evangelisation is an invitation to acknowledge the saving power at work in their lives and to put them at the centre of the Church's pilgrim way.[126]

Our Church communities need to go through this conversion to the poor. The dignity of the poor should be respected above all in the Church, in our liturgical assemblies and ecclesial groups. The poor need to feel at home, welcomed and not just tolerated. James chided the early Christians about being selective in concern for others and favouring some in the community over others:

> For if a person with gold rings and in fine clothes comes into your assembly, and if a poor person in dirty clothes also comes in, and if you take notice of the one wearing the fine clothes and say, 'Have a seat here please', while to the one who is poor you say, 'Stand there', or, 'Sit at my feet', have you not made distinctions among yourselves, and become judges with evil thoughts? ..Has not God chosen the poor in the world to be rich in faith and to be heirs of the kingdom that he promised to those who love him? (James 2:1-5)

Helping in Solidarity with the Poor

The Church is committed to come to the aid of the poor. Pope Paul VI stressed that our mission is to the whole human being, not just to the "soul".[127] We are not just about "saving souls", but the whole person. Giving of our substance is a necessary part of the proclamation of the gospel. John Chrysostom preached that "not to enable the poor to share in our goods is to steal from them and deprive them of life. The goods we possess are not ours, but theirs".[128] Pope Gregory the Great said, "When we attend to the needs of those in want, we give them what is theirs, not ours. More than performing works of mercy, we are paying a debt of justice".[129] Almsgiving to the poor has always been a sign of genuine following of Jesus. In our evangelising work we need to cultivate a generous heart of giving.

However, being for the poor is not only almsgiving. The Church hears the cry of the poor and out of love for humankind must respond. Working for social justice is an integral part of the proclamation of the good news. Pope Francis says, "None of us can think we are exempt from concern for the poor and for social justice".[130] He continues:

> In this context we can understand Jesus' command to his disciples: 'You yourselves give them something to eat'(Mk 6:37): it means working to eliminate structural causes of poverty and to promote the integral development of the poor, as well as small daily acts of solidarity in meeting the real needs which we encounter.[131]

Primacy of the Spiritual Mission

Yet we need to heed the warning of Pope John Paul II that we don't confuse the Church's mission with economic development. He says, "Her mission consists essentially in offering people an opportunity not to "have more" but to "be more" by awakening their consciences to the gospel". He wanted to underline that authentic human development must be rooted in bringing people to spiritual conversion. He wanted to redefine the concept of development, so that it is not simply seen as economic growth and technological advancement, as it is usually thought of in a consumerist society. Rather, genuine human development attends to the whole person. The primary activity of the Church is a spiritual mission.[132] The gospel brings conversion of heart first, and consequently recognition of the dignity of each person, solidarity with the poor, and commitment to one's neighbor, so that everyone has a place in God's plan.

Do Not Forget the Poor

That having been said, we will not be true friends of the poor if we are indifferent to their social and economic oppression. Pope Francis calls for a new mind-set which must come with our conversion to the poor. It recognises that private property is not an absolute value. We need a new conviction that the goods given to us by God on this planet are meant to be shared by all, and that goods privately owned should not be greedily amassed, but should be held for the common good of all. He quotes the bishops of South America, protesting for their own people:

> Seeing their poverty, hearing their cries and knowing their sufferings, we are scandalised because we know that there is enough food for everyone and that hunger is the result of a poor distribution of goods and income. The problem is made worse by the generalised practice of wastefulness.[133]

Meeting with government ministers from many countries and CEOs of the largest companies in the world, Pope Francis made a heartfelt appeal:

> Do not forget the poor! Do not be afraid to open your minds and hearts to the poor. In this way, you will give free rein to your economic talents, and discover the happiness of a full life, which consumerism of itself cannot provide. We must never allow the culture of prosperity to deaden us, to make us incapable of feeling compassion at the outcry of the poor, of weeping for other people's pain, and of sensing the need to help them, as if this was someone else's responsibility and not our own.[134]

Meeting Spiritual Needs

Even though the call for social justice is pressing, we must not let these concerns squeeze out our primary passion, the proclamation of the good news for spiritual conversion. Moving amongst the poor of this world it is obvious that the deepest need is spiritual consolation and the empowering that comes from the gospel itself. Like everyone else, no matter how desperate their circumstances, and indeed because of this desperation, what they long for most is the hope which comes from the saving love of God in Jesus Christ. In our godless world we can be duped into downplaying or even being cynical about bringing a spiritual message into such a depleted material situation. But those who move amongst the poor will discover that such negativity is not shared by the people. Pope Francis, who knows firsthand the poverty of developing countries laments "that the worst discrimination which the poor suffer is the lack of spiritual care".[135] These are the people who so often are most open to the good news, desiring to grow in faith, eager for the word of life, and ready to celebrate joyfully in the Spirit. "Our preferential option for the poor must mainly translate into a privileged and preferential religious care".[136]

The challenge is for the Church to penetrate into the darkest slum districts of the big cities of the world and bring "the good news to the poor". While this may seem a frightening mission full of potential danger for the evangelist, Pope Francis says:

> I prefer a Church which is bruised, hurting and dirty because it has been out on the streets, rather than a Church which is unhealthy from being confined and from clinging to its own security.[137]

We need to be moving amongst the poorest of the poor, touching the suffering flesh of Jesus, listening to the cries of those who may have been discarded by the society, seeking to bring hope to their hearts. We know that wealth and material comfort do not of themselves bring true happiness. In fact, if made absolute, they lead towards captivity and dehumanising behavior. On the other hand we know that, regardless of circumstances, the gospel brings light to the mind and hope to the heart which can be found nowhere else. We will find ourselves making friends with the homeless, prostitutes, drug addicts, and others on the margins of the society. The peace that every human heart seeks can only be found in Jesus. We may have a global vision for evangelisation but this will only be attained by meeting with love each individual person and drawing this one into relationship with the only Saviour, Jesus Christ, our Lord.

14
NEW EXPRESSIONS AND METHODS

THE DIGITAL WORLD

The so-called "digital revolution" in this era is impacting communication even more dramatically than the invention of the printing press in the 16th century. Communication devices are quickly becoming more powerful, smaller, more connected and accessible. The new media is relatively cheap. It costs little or nothing to launch a social media account or post a video online. A whole communication network can be effectively established from your bedroom. There's no need for an expensive studio and TV cameras. The new media is also widely accessible. Listeners don't have to turn up to a hall or watch a TV show at a particular time. Now anything posted on the internet is available 24/7 across the world.

Furthermore, the new media puts the Church in contact with people who would never dream of attending Mass or coming to a parish function. Yet they may well be engaged on Facebook and discuss deeply spiritual topics. They can watch thousands of Christian videos on YouTube or subscribe to blogs and tweets, while remaining safely anonymous before their computer screens. Non-Catholics can be quietly exploring the Catholic Church without having to face embarrassing questions from friends or become alienated from family or friends. This becomes a great opportunity for the new evangelisation.

When we speak about taking the gospel to the "ends of the earth" we need to remember the so-called "digital continent". As Pope Benedict reminded us, "The digital environment is not a parallel or purely virtual world, but is part of the daily experience of many people, especially the young".[138] For the new generation the digital devices are not just instruments to be used but are part of the fabric of their lives. The connectivity facilitated by these devices enables them to live in a context of networks of friendships, association and community that we could not have imagined a few decades ago. This new world of communication has become their fundamental point of reference for finding information and news, for self-expression, shaping public opinion, for dialogue and debate, and for forming relationships and community. We must find ways to communicate the gospel within this new culture. Otherwise the Church will be marginal to their lives and we will have missed a prime opportunity to bring the good news of Jesus.

An Interactive Medium

Bishop Robert Barron has been a leading evangelist in the digital world. He began uploading videos to YouTube in 2007. He thought it would be a great way to get his message out there for all to hear. If others can get thousands of viewers for cute babies or furry cats why not for the gospel? What he did not realise, however, was that YouTube is interactive. He was surprised to receive thousands of comments posted on his blog. Especially young people in their twenties and thirties responded to him, most of them anti-religion, and anti-Catholic. This provided him with a wonderful opportunity of reaching a whole demographic of people with whom otherwise it would have been impossible to engage. Bishop Barron testifies:

> I have an opportunity I would have in no other way, namely,

to engage people who would never dream of coming to any of the institutions of the Catholic Church... Many of them are sincere seekers who, perhaps to their great surprise, find themselves in dialogue with a priest in regard to some of the deeper questions.[139]

Bishop Barron has communicated the gospel through books of theology and spirituality, taught courses in seminaries, lectured business and civic leaders, and published dozens of articles in journals. But he says, "I believe that the most effective work I've done in this arena is through the internet."[140]

How we proclaim the good news on social media is important. It is a new way of communication that demands new approaches. Our presence in the digital world needs to recognise and respond to the distinctive culture of that environment. How can we best be authentic witnesses of our faith in this new arena? As Bishop Barron discovered, it is a strongly interactive medium. We need to humbly proclaim who we are and what we believe but always showing genuine concern for those we encounter, by listening to them, conversing respectfully with them and encouraging them. Rather than bombard people with "answers" we must take their questions seriously and allow them to fully express themselves.

A Culture of Encounter

When we are respecting people, avoiding any manipulation or malicious debate we are not only giving witness to our faith in Jesus, but also helping to humanise social media. We don't want to be enticed into acrimonious debates which perpetuate violence and division. That is the dark side of social media which we need to redeem. Rather than fall into that trap we need to promote an authentic culture of encounter. Pope Francis put it this way:

> We hold a precious treasure that is to be passed on, a treasure that brings light and hope…The great digital continent not only involves technology but is made up of real men and women who bring with them their hopes, their suffering, their concerns and their pursuit of what is true, beautiful and good. We need to bring Christ to others, through these joys and hopes, like Mary, who brought Christ to the hearts of men and women.[141]

When seeking to communicate the message on social media we can't just seek to broadcast a message and expect the public to passively consume it. Digital culture requires a more interactive participative approach. Digital communicators of the gospel need to be trained to engage in sharing the message in such a way that it invites a response and a respectful dialogue. Our views and ideas will not gain much traction unless we are willing to enter into dialogue. As Pope Francis says:

> We have to be able to dialogue with the men and women of today....We are challenged to be people of depth, attentive to what is happening around us and spiritually alert. To dialogue means to believe that the "other" has something worthwhile to say, and to entertain his or her point of view and perspective.[142]

The digital world also challenges us to avoid relying too much on text alone. It is a medium demanding images, video, music and gestures. Here especially the gift of art, music and dramatic expression can communicate the gospel more effectively. The new generation will be less likely to read, and more likely to listen to a story. But they will be even more likely to watch a video clip since they are now more visually inclined. Of course, we will need to speak, but when we do so we need to rediscover simple language, accessible metaphors, inspiring stories, and engaging bodily gestures.

THE WAY OF BEAUTY: ARTISTIC CREATIVITY

The Church has always revered creative artists, and has honoured their contribution to evangelisation. One has only to visit the Sistine Chapel and gaze upon Michelangelo's Last Judgement or enter any of the great cathedrals, such as Chartres and Notre Dame in France, to see how the whole message of salvation was proclaimed visually in an age when most of the lower classes were illiterate. The story was told through the architecture itself, by the stain glass windows, the frescoes, mosaics, and the icons, paintings and sculptures.

As a Church, to become more evangelical does not mean focusing on proclaiming the word alone. Go to evangelical Protestant churches and they are devoid of images, often with a raised pulpit from which the word is proclaimed. The cross will be found hanging on the wall but with no figure on it. All is devoted solely to the word from scripture preached from on high. To the contrary, the Catholic experience has always been incarnational. The Word became flesh. He did not come to diminish his creation, but to enhance and elevate it.

Catholicism involves the body and the senses as much as the soul and the mind. The spiritual realities are mediated through material things. Grace comes to us in a uniquely privileged way through the sacraments of the Church in which elements such as water, oil, bread and wine are taken into the sphere of the divine and used to communicate spiritual realities. Music, song, movement, gestures and incensing of the altar, the host and holy images take place in liturgies celebrated in cathedrals crafted by Catholic architects, artists and labourers. All of this engages us in the ongoing experience of the incarnation in the life of the Church. Also, in a broader more diffuse way, God's presence is mediated to us through the whole of his creation. So, when artists use created realities to express something of life, love and beauty they help us appreciate the beauty of God. In our churches the beautiful music, the glorious singing, the moving paintings, frescoes and mosaics, the dramatic presentations of the gospel, the processions, Eucharistic devotions, all help us to be bodily engaged with all our senses and to celebrate the fullness of life which is found in God.

Beauty Stirs the Soul

The Church needs poets, writers, painters, icon writers, architects, musicians, singers, actors, play writers, composers. And artists need the Church, since genuine artistic expression is by nature a spiritual activity. We proclaim the gospel through artistic medium. This is the way of beauty. We don't only proclaim that God is good and true, but that he is beautiful. Beauty wins the heart. Beauty stirs the soul to wonder and awe. Beauty is the key to encounter with the Mystery of God. The beauty of created things can never fully satisfy, since it is an invitation into communion with the Beauty of God. John Paul II invited all artists to accept this invitation: "Artists of this world, may your many different paths all lead to that infinite ocean of beauty where wonder becomes awe, exhilaration, unspeakable joy".[143] St Augustine, a lover of beauty, expressed it so well when his own love for beauty led him to God: "Late have I loved you, beauty, so ancient and so new; Late have I loved you!" As Dostoyevsky says, "beauty will save the world".[144]

Philosopher Peter Kreeft appeals to beauty in one pithy proof of God's existence:

> There is the music of Johann Sebastian Bach.
> Therefore there must be a God.
> You either see this or you don't.[145]

This is obviously not a rational argument for God, but many people resonate with this point. Why does entry into a classic gothic cathedral take our breath away? Why does gazing upon Rembrant's *Prodigal Son* stir us within the soul? Why do vast canyons, roaring waterfalls and mighty oceans leave us in awe? Why does listening to Bach's *St Matthews Passion* lift our spirits to another realm? Why do movies like *The Sound of Music* appeal so much that people come back again and again? It is because all of these experiences capture our ultimate yearning for God. God is ultimate beauty.

Beauty is Subversive

In 1999 Pope John Paul II gathered the artists of the world in the Sistine chapel and told them how much the Church needs artists:

> In order to communicate the message entrusted to her by Christ, the Church needs art. ...Art has a unique capacity to take one or other facet of the message and translate it into colours, shapes and sounds which nourish the intuition of those who look or listen. It does so without emptying the message itself of its transcendent value and its aura of mystery.[146]

In the post-modern imagination the awareness of God is asleep. All defences are guarded by the intellectual arguments of modern ideologies. But the human imagination can be awakened by beauty. Beauty is subversive. It slips under the radar of people's critical filters and arouses a response of the heart. If we revive the power of beauty and the arts within the Church then people's pre-conscious intuition and imagination will be excited. They will be surprised by the Spirit and opened to a new encounter with God. Pope Benedict concurs:

> In so far as it seeks the beautiful, fruit of an imagination which rises above the everyday, art is by its nature a kind of appeal to the mystery. Even when they explore the darkest

depths of the soul or the most unsettling aspects of evil, the artist gives voice in a way to the universal desire for redemption...Beauty can become a path towards the transcendent, towards the ultimate Mystery, towards God.[147]

In his Confessions, St Augustine affirmed "it is not possible to love what is not beautiful".[148] Beauty attracts us to love. Through our experience of beauty God reveals his face and we are drawn to love him. In this way artists, who are cooperating with the Creator in producing what is beautiful are "privileged communicators of the new evangelisation".[149] The Church today will fulfill its evangelising mission by enlisting creative artists to embody the message in ways that inspire and open the heart to the experience of wonder and awe before the reflected beauty of God.

INCULTURATION

We have already explored some of the ways the new evangelisation transforms culture. We looked at the challenges in Western secularist culture, the positive and negative aspects of the internet culture, the importance of all cultures pursuing beauty through the arts, and the need for faith communities to be developing a new culture of life and love. Pope Paul VI read the signs of the times accurately when he said:

> What matters is to evangelise human culture....The split between the gospel and culture is without doubt the drama of our time, just as it was of other times. Therefore every effort must be made to ensure a full evangelisation of culture.[150]

This drama is being played out differently now in a globalised world where instant communication is possible around the globe, and airline travel makes the "global village" more a reality. The danger is that distinctive cultures can lose their integrity. But we must remember that the Word was made flesh within a particular culture, that of Jewish heritage. Authentic inculturation of the Christian faith is grounded in the reality of the incarnation. God chose a particular people with a distinctive culture and made them his very own. He guided them towards the time when Jesus would be born, the Word made flesh. In affirming one culture, God affirmed all.

This means that the gospel can become incarnate in any culture. The Word made flesh is foreign to no culture and must be preached to all cultures. But we do not preach from on high as if God's word parachutes in from heaven above in a disembodied way. Rather, just as the Word was made flesh and dwelt amongst us, the gospel penetrates deeply into the life and culture of those who welcome its proclamation. Consequently, missionaries need to immerse themselves in the culture in which they work, learning the language and symbols of the culture and discovering its values. Only then can their proclamation be both enriching and purifying for the culture.

The gospel cannot be found outside of a particular culture, since it is always enfleshed within a culture. However, it is never bound by any culture. The gospel transcends culture. It can never be reduced to one culture, as if that is the privileged culture over all others. In the past European culture erroneously claimed that supremacy, but in our present age this hegemony has gone.

Dialogue with Culture

In previous eras missionaries often failed to insert themselves into the culture of the people to whom they were sent. Instead, missioning from Europe to other continents they brought not only the gospel but also European ecclesiastical culture, imposing this upon the locals, with little respect for the native culture. There were of course notable exceptions, such as the Jesuit Matteo Ricci in China, who learnt the language, observed interests, attitudes and behaviours, and then sought to inculturate the gospel. Ricci did not try to impose Western customs on the Chinese. Adapting to national customs he mastered the Chinese language, acquainted himself with the literary tradition and the etiquettes of the Chinese culture. All of this was to win hearts. By teaching mathematics and science he endeared himself to the Mandarins, high officials of the Empire, and the Confucian scholars. He even, somewhat controversially, donned a habit much like that of a Buddhist monk. The people experienced him as one of them, and consequently were open to the gospel he preached. Pope Francis recently expressed his admiration for Ricci who had entered into dialogue with the Chinese culture, being the first Westerner to gain entry into the Forbidden City. "Encounter", said the Pope, "is achieved through dialogue".[151] Dialogue does not mean compromise, but is based on genuine respect for the culture of the other, and willingness to learn from this culture. It creates opportunities for proclamation.

A New Missionary Situation

After the "new world" was discovered in the 16th century, the Church's missionary vision distinguished between "sending" countries and "receiving" countries. The former were the bearers of enlightenment. The latter were considered passive recipients of the gospel being brought to them. Now we are in a totally new situation where every people group is both a "sending" and a "receiving" body. In Australia, for example, to proclaim the gospel to the ends of the earth is not just to send missionaries to other nations with the good news. The other nations have come to us. Walk down any inner city street in Sydney and within a few blocks you have passed people from more than twenty different cultural backgrounds. Evangelising in our own backyard will involve respecting one another's cultures and allowing the fruits of the gospel to be manifest in each culture. In each culture the Christian faith will be lived in a unique way. The living word of Jesus will be expressed in ways that speak to the minds and hearts of this particular cultural grouping. In an intriguing turn of fortunes, the spiritually impoverished Australian Church is now being revitalised by immigrants from many ethnic groups which have a renewed faith, and a new energy for bringing the good news.

Inculturation of the Gospel

Writing to the Church in Oceania, Pope John Paul II affirmed that "authentic human culture has a double aspect".[152] On the one hand a culture will have positive values and forms which can be used to proclaim the gospel, to understand and live it. "The Christian faith affirms all that is genuinely human, while rejecting what is sinful". The process of inculturation involves a dialogue with the culture, seeking "to identify what is of Christ and what is not of Christ".[153] Every culture will have elements that need purification by the gospel, but keen discernment is needed, not jumping to conclusions too quickly from a stance of ignorance rather than a genuine understanding of the culture. The Pope encourages us to discover what is positive in the cultures of Oceania which "will enrich the way the gospel is preached, understood and lived".[154]

The many cultures of the region of Oceania form a rich and diverse communion. The various cultures provide ways the Church can better express the gospel. Although occasionally some experiments in this regard have missed the mark. Who should be the judge of this? In terms of what is culturally sensitive, the people themselves are the best judge. But in terms of what is true to the gospel and the Catholic faith the pastors of the Church need to be the judge. All evangelising, no matter where it happens, or with whom, is a work of the Church. Ultimately new expressions need to be tested whether they genuinely express the universal Catholic faith.[155]

The Gospel in Indigenous Culture

Pope John Paul II applied the principles of inculturation to the indigenous people of Australia when he gave his unforgettable speech to the Aboriginal and Torres Strait Islanders in Alice Springs in 1986:

> The gospel of our Lord Jesus Christ speaks all languages. *It esteems and embraces all cultures.* It supports them in everything human and, when necessary, it purifies them. Always and everywhere the gospel uplifts and enriches cultures with the revealed message of a loving and merciful God. *That gospel now invites you to become, through and through, Aboriginal Christians.*[156]

The Pope told the indigenous people that they don't need to feel divided within themselves, as though they had to borrow and put on Christianity like a hat or a pair of shoes, which are owned by someone else. By accepting the words and values of Jesus into their own culture they will become even more truly aboriginal. He encourages them to take the gospel into their own language and ways of communicating; to let it bring new strength to their stories and ceremonies. "The Church" he said, "invites you *to express the living word of Jesus in ways that speak to your Aboriginal minds and hearts".*[157]

> As you listen to the gospel of our Lord Jesus Christ, seek out the best things of your traditional ways. If you do, you will come to realise more and more, *your great human and Christian dignity*...Your Christian faith calls you to become the best kind of Aboriginal people you can be. This is possible only if reconciliation and forgiveness are part of your lives. Only

then will you find happiness. Only then will you make your best contribution to all your brothers and sisters in this great nation. You are part of Australia and Australia is part of you. *And the Church herself in Australia will not be fully the Church that Jesus wants her to be until you have made your contribution to her life and until that contribution has been joyfully received by others.*[158]

15
THE POWER OF INTERCESSION

The new evangelisation will be powered by prayer. When Elijah prayed, the long drought was broken, the heavens opened and rain poured down on a thirsty land. James comments, "The prayer of a righteous man is powerful in its effects" (James 5: 16-17). In the secularised desert of the modern world we have to depend on the power of God unleashed by faithful and persevering prayer to bring a change of heart. For our ministry to be anointed by the Spirit, all our works of evangelisation will need to be undergirded by intercession. The Holy Spirit will be poured out like new rain to thirsting souls to the degree that we ask God for this to happen, and put ourselves on the line with constant intercession on behalf of the lost.

To intercede, from the Latin *intercedere*, means to "stand between". We stand between God and those for whom we pray, and plead on their behalf. We are advocates for those who desperately need God's intervention. It is a step beyond ordinary petitionary prayer. When we petition God for something we ask specifically for a need that we have or a need that someone else has. This is a laudable prayer that should always be offered to the Lord. But intercession takes us further. While in petition God does something *for* us; in intercession God does something *through* us. We become his instruments for his work in the world. Our persistent prayer of intercession is a way of cooperating with God's saving work in the world. When we intercede we share as co-workers with Christ in the redemption of the world. We are used to speaking about being Christ's hands and feet, his smile and mouth-piece for the world, but we sometimes overlook that through our intercessory prayer he uses us even more powerfully in his saving work. The Church must have preachers, teachers, prophets, confessors and martyrs, but without intercession their apostolic work will lack the power of the Spirit and the love of Christ which is the heart of the Church.

Standing in the Breach

A scriptural image for intercession is "to stand in the breach".[159] When a break or a gap has occurred between God and his people, an intercessor needs to stand before God and plead on their behalf. When the Israelites had sinned by worshipping a golden calf they were worthy of destruction by God. But we are told that Moses, God's chosen one, "stood in the breach before him" to prevent the disaster. His prayer was effective. The Hebrew word used for "intercede" is *paw-gah*, meaning "persistently coming in between". It is use in the famous text from Ezekiel where the Lord could not tolerate the sinfulness of the people but was looking for someone to take a position between him and the people. He was looking for an intercessor to work with him, since his heart is for the salvation of all, not their destruction. "And I sought for anyone among them who would repair the wall and stand in the breach before me on behalf of the land, so that I would not destroy it; but I found no one" (Ezek 22:3).

The image is of a breach in the wall of a city caused by the attacking enemy. That is where the greatest defence is needed. The Lord looks for someone who would wear the personal cost of standing in the breach and hold back the advancing enemy from destroying the city. The enemy will throw everything he has at that place of weakness where God's people are most vulnerable. The Lord is looking for someone to take a position to protect the people from the onslaught of the evil one. This is the calling of intercessors. They have a special gift from God to experience the urgency of praying for the salvation of others. Intercession is both a way of turning back the wrath of God, whose holiness cannot abide with sin, and also a critical defence against the attack of the enemy of our human nature, who seeks to destroy us. It is a call to be vigilant, as sentinels for the Lord, day and night keeping awake to pray.

> On your walls, Jerusalem, I set watchmen. Day or night they must never be silent. You who keep the Lord mindful must take no rest. Nor let him take rest till he has restored Jerusalem, and made her the boast of the earth (Is 62: 6-7).

Praying for Evangelisation

Intercession is not only about protection and defence. It is also about cooperating with God in strengthening and empowering the offensive work of evangelisation. It is more important for our mission than any planning, management, funding strategy, or leadership skills. It is based in an expectant faith that God will act when we persistently call upon him to do so. A popular image for intercession is the way a magnifying glass can focus the energy of the sun on a piece of paper and set it alight. Concentrated intercessory prayer is like that. Intercessors focus the power of God onto people and impossible situations through prayer. Intercessors become a lens of prayer for God to "bring fire to the earth".

We need to pray with the heart of Jesus, the Good Shepherd, and feel his deep desire for the salvation of all men and women. We are told, "When he saw the crowds he felt sorry for them because they were harassed and dejected, like sheep without a shepherd" (Lk 9:36). The word in Greek for "felt sorry" means that he was deeply moved in his stomach. To use a colloquial expression, he was "wrenched in his guts". As we experience the lostness of our present generation something of that same "gut wrenching" feeling needs to be in us. United with the same Christ who wept over Jerusalem because it would not accept its moment of visitation, we need to cry out for the people of our day, that they turn back to God before it is too late. We need to be praying constantly as well for all in the Church who need to be shaken out of apathy and indifference, and come to a new revelation of who Jesus is and what he has done for us. In the spiritual battle Paul urges the Ephesians, "Pray all the time, asking for what you need praying in the Spirit on every possible occasion. Never get tired of staying awake to pray for all the saints" (Eph 6:18).

Jesus, the Unique Mediator

Praying in union with Christ is not only being in touch with his heart revealed in the gospels, but also being united with him as the eternal High Priest in heaven. Hebrews tells us, "his power to save is utterly certain, since he is living for ever to intercede for all who come to God through him" (Heb 7:25). As God-man, Jesus stands between God and humanity in an absolutely unique way. As Paul tells us, "there is one mediator between God and humankind, Christ Jesus, himself human, who gave himself as ransom for all" (1Tim 2:5-6). The greatest act of intercession by Jesus was his death on the cross. He cried out "I thirst!" which was more than a physical reality. He thirsted for souls, and died for each one of us. "During his life on earth he offered up prayer and entreaty, aloud and in silent tears…and he submitted so humbly that his prayer was heard"(Heb 5:10). God the Father raised him from the dead and his intercession continues at the right hand of the Father that everyone be saved. The author of Hebrews, aware that Jesus not only expiated our sins but continues to intercede for us, urges us, "Let us therefore approach the throne of grace with boldness, so that we may receive mercy and find grace to help in time of need" (Heb 4:16).

Spiritual Warfare

Intercession is a way of spiritual warfare.[160] Paul warns us that the real battle for souls is not something we can see with our eyes or touch with our hands. There is an invisible battle in which a whole army of evil is attacking the Church and throwing every weapon possible against the work of evangelisation. The target is both those who seek to evangelise and those who may be opening up to receive the good news. Paul says, "Put God's armour on so as to be able to resist the devil's tactics. For it is not against human enemies that we have to struggle, but against the sovereignties and powers who originate the darkness of this world, the spiritual army of evil in the heavens" (Eph 6: 10-12). By intercession we jam the wavelengths of the evil spirits and undo the strategies of the enemy. In this battle we need to be convinced that Satan is a defeated foe. He has been vanquished once and for all by the victory of Christ through the cross and resurrection. When God the Father raised Jesus from the dead "he put all things under his feet" (Eph 1:22). "Thanks be to God who has given us the victory through our Lord Jesus Christ" (1Cor 15:17). In the prayer of intercession we claim this victory. We are confident that Jesus' promise to his Church is true, that "the gates of hell will not prevail against it" (Mt 16:18).

As we evangelise, we have to do battle with the strongholds of Satan, particularly those in the minds of people. Intercessory prayer in the Spirit is crucial for this. Paul tells us that it is as if a shroud has come over the minds of those who resist the gospel message. Prayer can lift the veil. He speaks of "unbelievers whose minds the god of this world has blinded to stop them seeing the light shed by the good news of the glory of Christ" (1Cor 4:4). Intercessory prayer is powerful to break these strongholds of the Evil One in the minds of people, so the light of Christ will break through the darkness and help them to see the truth that will set them free. Paul says that, in spiritual battle, the weapons we use are spiritual, not those of the flesh. They are strong enough to demolish "fortresses, sophistries, and the arrogance that tries to resist the knowledge of God" (2 Cor 10:4). We must preach the gospel, but it relies upon being backed up by persistent intercession. This is the way the kingdom of God will take hold in the world and the kingdom of darkness will be routed.

When the Israelites were attacked by the Amalekites at Rephidim, Moses commanded Joshua to lead the fighting on the plain. He did not join the thick of the battle, but took with him Aaron and Hur and they climbed a large hill overlooking the scene of the battle. Moses' purpose was to intercede. We are told, "As long as Moses kept his arms raised, Israel had the advantage; when he let his arms fall, the advantage went to Amalek" (Ex 17:8-16). As long as Moses, the leader of his people, had his arms raised in prayer Israel prevailed in the battle. It speaks of the necessity of intercession and its effectiveness in the spiritual battle. We would be naïve to blithely plan evangelising activities without accompanying intercession. The story continues that Moses would tire and his arms would sag, so he enlisted Aaron and Hur to support his arms so he could persevere in prayer and the victory could be claimed. This symbolises well the need for intercession to be done in groups if at all possible. The group dynamic helps to support one another under the burden of this demanding ministry.

Intercession in the Spirit

When groups come together to intercede for breakthroughs in evangelisation, or indeed for any purpose, the first task is to listen to the promptings of the Holy Spirit.[161] It is not about bringing a list of pre-prepared petitions. Rather it is a time to be open to the Lord, seeking to tap into what his concerns and plans are. The aim is to get in touch with the burdens on the heart of God, rather than to conjure up our own concerns. In this sense it can be called "prophetic intercession"; a prophet listens for the voice of God and acts from this. In Amos we are told, "The Lord God does nothing without revealing his mind to his servants the prophets" (Amos 3:7). The intercessors want to cooperate with God's plan and offer themselves to accomplish his plan through prayer; to be able to do this they must first listen, keep their eyes fixed on the Lord, and seek his heart.

This way of praying requires participants to first empty themselves of their own ideas, plans, and anxieties. They must come humbly open to the Lord's direction, and be available to the Holy Spirit. In his way they will be inspired to pray according to the Lord's will, which may be very different than what they originally expected. They need to place themselves in the hands of the Lord, making themselves like clay in the hands of the Potter. They aim to yield to the direction of the Spirit, and move in conformity with the will of God.

Keys to Intercession

Firstly each member of the group needs to come with a pure heart. This may well mean they have to repent. Intercessors are like an irrigation channel through which water from the dam can flow to bring good fruit. If the channel is blocked by sin then it is useless. They need to call on the cleansing of the precious blood of Jesus, and if necessary use the sacrament of Reconciliation. One of the blockages may be resentment, bitterness or unforgiveness. Jesus promised "everything you ask and pray for, believe that you have it already, and it will be yours". But he followed this up with a further injunction, "And when you stand in prayer, forgive whatever you have against anybody, so that your Father in heaven may forgive your failings too" (Mk 11:24-25). In a group it may be necessary to iron out any relational difficulties, or resolve any conflicts, before commencing the prayer. To pray in unity is critical. Jesus promised, "If two or three of you on earth agree to ask anything at all it will be granted to you by my Father in heaven. For where two or three meet in my name, I shall be there with them" (Mt 18: 19-20). If the group is divided by jealousies, rivalry or unresolved conflict its capacity to intercede will be severely impaired.

Secondly, intercessors need to move with the compassion and love of the heart of Jesus. They will feel the burdens for whom they are praying. Sometimes people with this gift are awakened in the middle of the night to pray for something which they sense is a burden on the heart of the Lord at this very moment. When Jesus arrived in Bethany after his friend Lazarus had died he was touched deeply by the faith of Martha and Mary who declared that if he had been present Lazarus would not have died. He was also moved by their tears. He himself wept at the tomb. In response to their pleas, and because he himself was burdened with loss of Lazarus he ordered the stone to be rolled away. Standing at the entrance to the tomb he prayed, "Father I thank you for hearing my prayer" and with loud voice he cried out, "Lazarus, come out!" The hearts of Martha and Mary were one with Jesus as they made their cries to him. Their intercession was an act of compassion and faith in the power of God.

In intercession we selflessly identify with the pain of others. It is like the pain of giving birth. Paul speaks of the whole world groaning in one great act of giving birth, and we too groan as we yearn for the redemption yet to come (Rom 8:23). Intercessors are often groaning in prayer. And when they cannot find the words to express their prayer, the Holy Spirit brings forth "groans too deep for words" (Rom 8: 27). In this regard the gift of tongues is particularly helpful in intercession, since no words are necessary but the sounds are produced by the Spirit within and in harmony with the heart of God.

Thirdly, as mentioned above, they need to give their agenda over to the Lord, and come with a surrendered mind and heart. They must be ready to listen to the Lord and then pray according to his will. They can begin by gently praying in tongues or just being silent before the Lord, opening their spirits to whatever the Lord would impress upon them. What is the Lord's heart in this matter? After a while of gently listening they may draw together the sense of what they believe the Lord is revealing to them. This is the prophetic dimension of the intercessory exercise. Then like good prophets they should act upon what they have heard by praying into those areas in a vigorous manner, claiming the victory of the Lord and rebuking the powers of darkness in the mighty name of Jesus. They should pray with great conviction, already thanking the Lord and praising him for his work in our midst. This is what Jesus instructs us to do, to "pray with no hesitation in your heart, believing that it has been granted already".

Fourthly, they will pray with confidence and perseverance. As mentioned above, intercessors are given expectant faith. Having listened to what they believe is the will of God, they then pray with great confidence that this will be achieved. Jesus said, "If you ask for anything in my name I will do it" (Jn 14:14). Thus, we pray with utter trust in the Lord. We also pray with perseverance. Jesus' parables about prayer emphasise persistence, never to give up. The man who was knocking on the door of his neighbour for bread, when they had already bedded down for the night, had only to persist and his neighbour would eventually open the door (Lk 11:5-13). We too have only to persevere, make a pest of ourselves before God, and he will eventually come through with what we ask. Similarly, the widow demanding her just rights before a corrupt judge was ignored, but Jesus says if she continues to disturb him she will get results. The frustrated judge says to himself, "since she keeps pestering me I must give this widow her just rights, or she will persist in coming and worry me to death". Jesus comments, "You notice what the unjust judge has to say? Now will not God see justice done to his chosen who cry to him day and night even when he delays to help them?" (Lk 18:1-8)

Therese and Catherine

Sometimes when interceding we feel we must present every detail of a situation to the Lord, forgetting that he knows already those details and even more about what we are asking or for whom we are praying. That doesn't mean we just have to wait patiently for the Lord to act. No, he loves us to cry out to him, since we are in the place of radical dependence before him. Yet, Therese of Lisieux, patroness of missionaries, whose life in a Carmelite convent was spent in the heart of the Church, praying for the spread of the gospel, had an intriguing insight. She felt herself captured by the words of the Lord from the Song of Songs, "Draw me in your footsteps, let us run…" (Song 1:3). By this she understood that it was just too tiring to enumerate all of the needs that she wanted to bring before the Lord. All she had to do was to follow him in her heart, and with all of her energy throw herself upon him with love, and everything else would be fine. "O Jesus, the soul who plunges into the shoreless ocean of your love, draws with her all the treasures she possesses". By "the treasures" she means all those who have been recommended to her for prayer.[162]

Catherine of Siena has another remarkable image for intercession. She used to picture herself standing at the foot of the cross of Jesus, collecting the blood shed for all humanity in a bowl, and casting the blood of Jesus onto hardened hearts. She was convinced that hearts which are "as hard as diamonds" will only be broken open by the power of his blood.[163] She would invoke the blood of Jesus, asking that those for whom she prayed would be utterly soaked in his blood, and hence not be able to resist the movement of his love and mercy for them.

The Blessed Virgin Mary and all the Saints

When interceding we are not alone. We are surrounded by "so many witnesses in a great cloud on every side of us" (Heb 12:1). This is both the pilgrim Church on earth, but also the communion of saints in heaven. They have gone before us. They know our struggles on this pilgrim journey. They are one with us, and we can enlist their prayers. Since they are so much closer to God, their intercession is so much more powerful. In the spiritual battle we can especially enlist Michael the Archangel who thrust Lucifer down to hell. In the traditional prayer to St Michael we ask him to "defend us in the hour of conflict" and "to be our protection against the wickedness and snares of the devil".

The greatest intercessor in Christ is the Blessed Virgin Mary, Queen of all saints. She is often depicted in statues with her foot crushing the head of the serpent, referring to the text in Genesis when God says to the Satan, "I will put enmity between you and the woman, and between your offspring. It will crush your head and you will strike its heel" (Gen 3:15). While the literal meaning is otherwise, tradition has seen this as referring to the Blessed Mother, as the new Eve crushing the head of Satan by her intercession. Biblical disputes aside, it holds as a great image of the power of Mary's intercession. We should ask her often to pray with us, just as she prayed with the apostles at the first Pentecost. The rosary is particularly powerful in intercession. We remember how, at the battle of Lepanto, the Christian fleet, supported by the whole of Europe, prayed the rosary for victory. Again an image for the spiritual battle. Often, like the Christian fleet facing the far superior Armada bearing down upon them, we find ourselves seemingly against impossible odds. The rosary prayed from the heart, calling upon the intercession of Mary, the Queen of Victories, is enormously effective.

Prayer and Fasting

Finally, we must say something about fasting. Undoubtedly "prayer and fasting" is a powerful means of intercession. Jesus fasted in the desert for forty days as a preparation for his mission of preaching the gospel (Lk 4:14). He ascribed special power to fasting. When the apostles had not been able to cast out an evil spirit from an epileptic boy, Jesus cast it out. The apostles later asked Jesus, "Why could we not cast it out?" One of the ancient sources has Jesus reply, "This kind can come out only with prayer and fasting" (Mk 9:29). We can use fasting to pray effectively for those who may be resistant to hearing the gospel message. We pray that the Lord will soften their hearts and the Holy Spirit will prepare the way for them to be able to hear the word, and be led to conversion.

It is clear that Jesus did not have the ascetical approach to fasting like John the Baptist. People noticed this and remarked about it. Jesus replied that while his disciples do not fast there will come a time when they will do so. That time will be "when the bridegroom is taken away from them" (Mk 2:14-22). Jesus did not want to establish a strict regime like that of the Essenes from where John probably came. The new wine of the Spirit needed new wineskins. In other words, now in the time of the Spirit, we must fast, not like John's disciples, but as a way of intercessory prayer led by the Holy Spirit.

Through fasting we express bodily our deep hunger for God, and our total reliance upon him to break through the hard hearts of those who have moved away from him. We express our utter need for God, and on behalf of those whom we are holding up to him, we make the plea with our bodies that they cannot make with their spirits. In putting our own bodies on the line we are crying out for their union with God. We make our bodies a living sacrifice to God for the sake of those for whom we intercede.

16
THE EVANGELISERS

We are all called to evangelise. But what are the qualities we need to develop to be effective evangelists? What are the attitudes we need to cultivate? What sort of spiritual outlook should evangelists have?

Called to be Apostles

Firstly, they must know they are apostles. An apostle is someone who knows he or she is sent to bring the good news of Jesus to others. It's no secret that in the Church many who are relatively committed disciples, are not yet committed apostles. They are not yet convinced of the need to bring the good news to others beyond the closed circle of their immediate community. They attend Mass regularly, participate in parish or ecclesial community activities, and hunger for on-going spiritual nourishment and support. But they still remain primarily spiritual consumers, keen for all that is offered, but not aware of the challenge to go beyond their comfort zone to reach out to others beyond the confines of their chosen community.

In reality people who have this perspective have not yet been fully evangelised themselves! They may have been adherents to the Church for many years, but they do not yet share the impulse of the Spirit to take the good news to others, and to welcome others into their midst. There is a serious deficiency in their own evangelisation. Pope Paul VI in his uncompromising way gave us what he called "the test of truth, the touchstone of evangelisation". The test of whether evangelisation has fully happened is not just that a person comes to know Jesus personally and participates in the sacramental life of the Church. These are great outcomes, but they are meant to overflow into evangelising activity. The Pope says, "It is unthinkable that a person should accept the Word and give himself to the kingdom without becoming a person who bears witness to it and proclaims it in his turn".[164] Genuine discipleship cannot be separated from being an apostle. Any community in the Church needs to have contagious apostolic fervour so that those who belong to it know that membership means not only spiritual feeding, but also reaching out beyond the community within their own personal sphere of influence to invite others into the banquet of life.

Not Only the Specialists

In talking about evangelists, or apostles, I want to underline we are not only referring to specialists who have been trained for this purpose as priests, religious, and full-time lay pastoral workers. We are talking about all members of the Church. In many ways the professional qualifications don't matter, even though acquiring knowledge and skills is very useful. But without the qualities of an evangelist they will be of little real use. In other words, we are all called to be effective evangelists in our own spheres of influence; those in business with their work colleagues, students with their fellow students, carpenters with their mates on the building site, teachers with their students, and spouses at home with their children, and whoever they meet at the school canteen or sporting events. So what are these qualities of the evangelist? I am relying mainly on Pope Francis, and would give the disclaimer that the list is far from complete.

Guided by the Spirit

"Evangelisation will never be possible without the action of the Holy

Spirit...The Holy Spirit is the principal agent of evangelisation".[165] Everything must be soaked in the Holy Spirit, especially the one who evangelises. Spirit-filled evangelisers will be open to the Holy Spirit at all times. We will often be aware of our weakness and incapacity, but we will be trusting in the Spirit's work within us and in giving us what we need to say. At times we will feel discouraged and fearful, sometimes we will feel embarrassed and ridiculed by others. The Holy Spirit will be our strength. Paul cried in his weakness begging the Lord three times to take the "thorn in his side" away. He received the answer from the Lord, "My grace is enough for you; my power is at its best in weakness" (2Cor 12:9). Pope Francis himself admits that sometimes he has felt totally out of his depth and had to put his trust fully in the mysterious unseen working of the Spirit. He goes on to say, "Yet there is no greater freedom than allowing ourselves to be guided by the Holy Spirit, renouncing the attempt to plan and control everything to the last detail, and instead letting him enlighten guide and direct us, leading us wherever he wills".[166] He says that the Holy Spirit always knows what is best for us, and we can trust his mysterious movement. As Jesus said, "The wind blows where it chooses, and you hear the sound of it, but you do not know where it comes from or where it goes. So it is with everyone who is born of the Spirit" (Jn 3:8).

Boldness in the Spirit

The Holy Spirit also gives courage to evangelists to proclaim the gospel in a new way in every place and circumstance, no matter what opposition comes against them. This is the gift of "boldness", a translation of the New Testament Greek word, *parresia*. This word originated in ancient Greece where democracy was born. It spoke of the right of any citizen to speak anywhere in public places and the right to be heard. The first apostles at Pentecost received this gift. When Peter and John were hauled before the Sanhedrin for preaching courageously in the name of Jesus, they were ordered not to preach in the name of Jesus again. They responded fearlessly that it was impossible for them to stop proclaiming in the name of Jesus since "there is no other name under heaven given among mortals by which we can be saved" (Acts 4:12). The members of the Sanhedrin were utterly astonished at "the boldness of Peter and John, considering they were uneducated laymen" (4:13). Without any training in evangelisation, no theological education, these mere fishermen had acquired an extraordinary "boldness". They had been filled with the Holy Spirit. They knew they had the right to speak and the right to be heard, because it had been given them from God.

Becoming Contemplative: To Know and Love Jesus

When the Holy Spirit is active in our lives we have an intense desire to know and love Jesus more deeply. The Spirit glorifies Christ within us. Standing before a crucifix we are overwhelmed by the love of God. Paul tells us, "The love of Christ overwhelms us when we think that if one man died for all, all should have died..." (2Cor 5:14). We cannot be unmoved before the image of Jesus crucified. As we look upon him, whom we have pierced, the one whose heart was broken open in love for us, we find our own hearts broken open in love for him and for all men and women. We then "speak of what we have seen and heard" (1Jn 1:3). Contemplation of Jesus on the cross, and indeed of his whole life and ministry as related in the gospels is an irreplaceable preparation for evangelisation. We are "stewards of the mystery of Christ" and we need to first be captured by the mystery of his love to fulfil our task. We proclaim Jesus as the lasting treasure of our lives but we must first be like the man in the gospel parable who found the treasure. It filled him with such joy that he gave up everything to possess the treasure. This same joy is meant to be ours; and it is with this joy that we offer the "priceless pearl" of Christ to others.

Here we need to briefly allude to a major obstacle to developing a contemplative spirit – the internet! I have already spoken of the immense opportunity for communication that the internet brings. However, unfortunately some become enslaved to its demands. The screen of the computer or smartphone opens up a world undreamed of only a few years ago. You can flit from one site to another, check out the social media as you desire, download something of interest. What a wonderful instrument for instant information from across the globe! The paradox is that while it feels like we are gaining more freedom in fact we can be seduced into passivity, a form of captivity. We get hooked. Recently experts have discovered that the constant distractions that the internet offers affect us at a neurological level. The brain alters itself to get accustomed to this nonstop, random, stimuli. We become conditioned to crave repetitive "hits" with each novelty presented to us. Our mental circuits get rewired by this constant flood of stimulating experiences.

Disturbingly, since the plasticity of the brain of young people is so much more susceptible to heavy doses of stimuli, they are more prone to be hooked, and develop a life-time addiction. This seriously affects our ability to pay attention, to focus and to think deeply. Consequently, the internet can be a serious obstacle to learning contemplation. The iPhone promises the world, but used wrongly it can take us captive. We need to be alert to the dangers of social media, not just because there is a fair level of voyeurism operating, but because the medium is actually altering the way we experience the world and interpret it. Unless handled maturely, the Church could lose its capacity for spiritual depth and nourishment. Nothing is more important to the Church than prayer. It is ironic that the very instrument that promises such wonderful new opportunities for communication, unless used wisely, could rob us of our capacity for deep encounter with God and with one another!

For the new evangelisation to be true fire to the earth it will need to be proclaimed by people who know the fire of God's love through hours of silent prayer before Jesus in the Blessed Sacrament. Great words arise out of silence, and return to silence. Jesus himself went aside often to be alone with the Father; he was constantly tapping into the Father's heart. We need time to be aside with Jesus in the Blessed Sacrament. This must be highest priority for any evangelist. In the quiet we give him permission to penetrate our hearts with his love, and slowly we become more like him. Over time we discover a change is taking place. We have a new power to love him and to love others; we have a new fire to proclaim the good news of his love. To spend time with the Beloved is to become like the Beloved.

A Deep Conviction of the Truth

The Holy Spirit in our lives will bring a strong conviction that the deepest answer to the cry for love in every heart is found in Jesus, and that the deepest quest for truth in every heart will find its fulfilment in Jesus. As Pope John Paul II said:

> The missionary is convinced that, through the working of the Spirit, there already exists in individuals and peoples an expectation, even if an unconscious one, of knowing the truth about God, about humanity, and about how we are to be set free from sin and death. The missionaries' enthusiasm in proclaiming Christ comes from the conviction that he is responding to that expectation.[167]

This conviction needs to be again and again awakened in us since our secularised culture within which we move daily has a dulling effect on the mind and saps the heart of enthusiasm for the gospel. This does not happen necessarily by any outward violence, but by an insidious negativity towards expecting anything supernatural to be at all significant for human living. We need to work constantly on a life of contemplative prayer where we experience the loving gaze of Jesus upon us and open our hearts in love for him. If we do not know the absolute need in our own hearts for the saving, liberating presence of Jesus, we will not have sufficient conviction to share about him to others. As Pope Francis eloquently proclaimed:

> It is impossible to persevere in a fervent evangelisation unless we are convinced from personal experience that it is not the same thing to have known Jesus as not to have known him, not the same thing to walk with him as to walk blindly, not the same thing to hear his word as not to know it, and not the same thing to contemplate him, to worship him, to find our peace in him, as not to. It is not the same thing to try to build the world with his gospel as to try to do so by our own lights.[168]

Jesus must be at the centre of our evangelising efforts. Otherwise it is doomed to failure. An evangelist who is not in love with Jesus, who is not fully convinced that Jesus is the answer to the deepest questions of life, who is not certain and enthusiastic about the treasure of Christ who is proclaimed, will not convince anyone.

Belonging to a Faith Community

Evangelists will always belong to a lived community and will go out from and return to this community. The Holy Spirit always draws us out of isolation into communion with others, and moves us from independence to interdependence with others. In our modern individualistic society the ideal is to go it alone and make your own way through life with your close family and just a few favoured friends. The consumer mentality fosters provisional commitment to any local community, whether it be a parish community or a new ecclesial community. People often tend to choose what suits them for as long as it meets their perceived needs, and then move on to another connection. Others need to move about due to work demands, finding a suitable house, and other economic or social factors in an increasingly mobile society. In this fluid society we Christians have to work hard not to be robbed of genuine community. If we are going to take the risk of evangelising we need a stable community base by which our faith can be nurtured, we can receive solid teaching, and we can be supported in the struggle to share the gospel.

Pope Francis encourages us not to fall into the trap of allowing internet and social media communication to rob us of personal encounter. He says it is not enough to communicate by screens and systems that can be turned on and off on command. Personal relationships are more mysterious and more demanding than that. The gospel challenges us "to run the risk of a face-to-face encounter with others, with their physical presence which challenges us, with their pain and their pleas, with their joy which infects us in our close and continuous interaction".[169] He encourages us not to flee from the challenge of personal, committed relationships. In the Church we need to learn to be vulnerable with one another and not hide from one another, and not to flit conveniently from one place to another, avoiding creating "deep and stable bonds".[170] He counsels that the only way to encounter others with a good attitude is to accept them non-judgementally and esteem them as companions on the way. "Better yet" he says "it means learning to find Jesus in the faces of others, in their voices, in their pleas". This means sharing in the suffering of Jesus in the other and "never tiring of our decision to live in fraternity".[171]

A Community which Shows the Face of Christ

Evangelists need to be committed within a community which is itself missionary in focus. It's too difficult to be a "lone ranger" evangelist. You can easily be picked off by the forces of darkness. As a community together we are able to witness by our way of life to the love of Jesus. We have a lived reality of Church to bring people to experience. Like Andrew, when he went to his brother Peter, we can say to people, "we have found Jesus" and invite them to "come and see". We trust they will discover Christ incarnate in the new way of life that the community is living. Our communities may be only a "little flock" (Lk 12:32), but they will be warm and hospitable places where the Christian life can be seen lived in all its simplicity and beauty. These communities are meant to be the salt of the earth and the light of the world (Mt 5:13-16). All of our talk about Christ will only make sense when people find him incarnate in our way of life within a loving community. Our communities are meant to cultivate a culture of face to face relationships, a culture of encounter, where everyone is known and loved, and where the "revolution of tenderness" is taking place. In the harsh, conflictual, environment of our modern societies, people can find in community a haven of peace and sense of acceptance, belonging, and care, for which every heart longs.

A Love for All People

Evangelists, because they love Jesus, will also find in their heart a love for all people and a profound respect for each individual. Indeed the one who does not love others "walks in darkness" (1Jn 3:14). "God is love and anyone who lives in love lives in God" (1Jn 4:16). Indeed, if I close my heart, even partly, to another person to that degree I have closed my heart to God. We need to evangelise not so much by argumentation but by love, and when words are spoken we will speak the truth in love. Our love for Jesus means that we will draw near to others; we will want to live at the heart of his people. The true missionary gains the greatest joy in reaching out to others and helping them in whatever way serves at this moment. Love is desiring the best for the other and doing something about it. "It is more blessed to give than to receive" (Acts 20:35). Locking ourselves up in our comforts, or hiding behind our computer, or refusing to share ourselves with those in need, is the way of death. The way of life is the way of giving of oneself for the sake of others. It is the way of sacrificial love.

Pope Francis encourages us to take seriously that as sons and daughters of God through Baptism we are all missionaries. He says this identity is not something we can shrug off; it is not an "extra" to our lives, not something superfluous which we could throw off as if it wouldn't matter. Being missionary is fundamental to who we are as baptised Catholics. He says it this way:

> I am a mission on this earth; that is the reason why I am here in this world. We have to regard ourselves as sealed, even branded, by the mission of bringing light, blessing, enlivening raising up, healing and freeing.[172]

The Pope is not just talking about his role as pope, or bishop or priest. He is talking about the seal of baptism, by which each of us has been marked out by God to be a missionary; to bring love to others. This is the reason we are on the planet.

Being at the heart of the people means that we have a particular love for the poor. Sometimes, he says, "we are tempted to be that kind of Christian who keeps the Lord's wounds at arm's length. Yet Jesus wants us to touch human misery, to touch the suffering flesh of others. He hopes that…we will enter into the reality of other people's lives and know the power of tenderness".[173] We will believe completely in the intrinsic value of every person, rejoicing with those who rejoice, weeping with those who weep, bringing hope to those who may be despairing. We will go to the fringes where people may have lost their way, but we will make companions with them without a hint of condemnation, nor any interior sense of superiority. We offer unconditional acceptance and the hope that comes from Jesus.

Courage in the Battle

Our evangelising mission in today's world requires courage beyond the ordinary. We are literally on a rescue mission in a battlefield where many wounded need help. The image that comes to mind is that of Private Dawson in the popular movie, *Hacksaw Ridge*. Dawson, whose real name was Desmond Goss, had enlisted in the American army to serve in the Second World War, but refused to bear arms. A deeply committed Christian, he wanted to fight in a way that would save people. Despised and reviled by his fellow soldiers, he faced a tough time in the barracks, but he stood firm in determination to be a medic and not even touch a gun. Against all opposition and derision, he was given the clearance to enter the theatre of war with no weapon. It was well known in the Pacific war that the Japanese were targeting medics to reduce morale; many medics took off their red crosses and blended into the regular troops. Not Desmond Goss! He wanted to minister to the wounded under the sign of the cross of Christ.

His greatest hour was in the decisive battle for Okinawa Island in May 1945. The advance of the 77th Division had hit a wall, a seemingly impregnable cliff face called Hacksaw Ridge. The American soldiers landing on the beach faced a sheer rock cliff, ten to twenty metres high. After many assaults they were turned back again and again by the Japanese who had heavily fortified the cliff with pill boxes and a system of caves within which they were able to shelter. During a lapse in the fighting the Americans managed to set up a rope cargo net hanging down the cliff, which would enable men to scramble up to the top quickly; but even this was not proving successful. The enemy positions were dug in so well that it seemed impossible to overcome. In the midst of this savage fighting there were many casualties. Desmond simply moved around in the midst of open fire tending to the wounded, and carrying them to safety. He would not only carry out men who had some possibility of surviving, but also those who most likely would die anyway.

A turning point in the battle came when the Americans managed to throw grenades into a pill box which ignited the Japanese weapons cache, causing a series of huge explosions throughout their caves. This brought the Japanese to the surface and they mounted a ferocious counter attack in which hundreds of Americans died or were wounded and sent survivors clambering back down the cargo net to the beach. Only one man remained at the top – Desmond Goss. He knew that the Japanese often tortured the wounded at night time. He had a couple of hours to try to save as many of his wounded comrades as he could. He cried out to the Lord, and felt the call not to retreat but to stay in the battle. He walked back into the enemy fire and began seeking out the wounded.

One by one Desmond would minister a pain-killer to wounded men and then lift them up or drag them to the edge of the cliff. Then he remembered how as a boy he learnt how to make a bow-line knot which would work for him to hitch each man by rope and lower him down to the soldiers below. The soldiers at the bottom could hardly believe what they were seeing; again and again a seriously wounded soldier was being lowered down for medical treatment. Each time Desmond would get a man safely down to the bottom he would head back into the line of fire to pick up another one. And each time he would pray, "Lord, please help me get one more". Miraculously he was not shot. One of the Japanese testified after the war that more than once he had Goss in his sights but when he went to pull the trigger his gun jammed. Seventy five men owe their lives to Desmond's saving work done single-handedly. No one would ever forget such bravery.

This is a driving principle for our evangelising. The Church is a field hospital in a battle ground. We need dedicated men and women who will not be phased by the intensity of the battle, but keep calm with the peace of Christ. Like Desmond Goss they will draw their strength from the power of prayer, the word of God, and the Holy Spirit. Their prayer will be "Lord, please help me get one more". One more person coming into contact with the healing love of Jesus, one more person being rescued from Satan's grip from addictive patterns of sin, one more person saved from emptiness, anguish and hopelessness, one more person given the breath of new life that comes from Christ, one more person finding clarity of purpose in the confusion of modern philosophies, one more person finding the exhilarating joy of Christ, one more person finding their true vocation in the Lord.

With Joy and Hope

Evangelists should always be joyful! We can be robbed of our joy if we start to become over-protective of ourselves, worried about the cost of reaching out to others, and making inordinate time for our own relaxation. This is a fleshy withdrawal from anything too painful or requiring too much sacrifice. We become too focussed on our own needs for comfort and satisfaction. True joy is found in giving until it hurts, rather than in inordinate self-preservation. We can also lose our joy if we place unrealistic expectations on ourselves, measuring the value of our evangelising by the lack of immediate results. Rather than being patient and trusting in the Lord we can fall into disappointment and disillusionment. Joy comes when we give the work of conversion over to the Lord and stop thinking that it all depends on us.

Jesus promised he would give us a joy which cannot be taken away from us (Jn 16:22). We need to be realistic optimists, not dismayed by the encroaching evil around us or by the way so many seem impervious to the gospel. As Pope John Paul II reminded us,[174] Peter and the apostles had been fishing all night and caught nothing when Jesus told Peter to put out into the deep for a catch. Peter could have sullenly ignored Jesus' command. After all Peter was a fisherman and he knew there were no fish biting that morning. But he obeyed the Lord, threw out the nets, and they had an overwhelming catch (cf Lk 5:1-11). Our situation is often similar. The catch doesn't ultimately depend on us, but on the Lord.

Evangelists can be robbed of their hope. We must resist that. The ploy of the evil spirit is to knock us out of the game by causing us to go down into a pit of discouragement. In the face of the opposition before us we are tempted to throw the towel in even before the battle has started. This attitude of defeatism stifles boldness and zeal. As Pope Francis says, "nobody can go off to battle unless he is fully convinced of victory beforehand".[175] The world we face today is certainly a challenging arena but it is no worse than what the early Christians faced as the set out to convert the mighty Roman Empire. The same Holy Spirit has been given to us for the same purpose. The victory over evil has already been won through the resurrection of Jesus. Any negative, pessimistic thinking needs to be overcome within us; we simply confess with our lips that Jesus is Lord and believe in our hearts that God raised him from the dead.

We are told that when the first disciples preached "the Lord worked with them and confirmed the message" (Mk 16:20). The same Lord will work with us also. We move ahead in resurrection power, not by our own strength. Paul wanted us to know "how infinitely great is the power that the Father has exercised for us believers". He says, "This you can tell from the strength of his power at work in Christ when he used it to raise him from the dead" (Eph 1:19-20). Our hope is in the risen Christ. And we can rely on the Holy Spirit. Jesus said, "You will receive power when the Holy Spirit comes upon you; then you will be my witnesses" (Acts 1:8). We can put our trust totally in the power of the Holy Spirit, who applies to our lives and to our ministry the victory of Jesus' resurrection. Even though we feel weak, inept, and ill-equipped against the sophisticated onslaught that can come against us, the Spirit "helps us in our weakness", and we will find that the Lord will bring about miracles of conversion that will astound us.

All for the Glory of God

Just before Jesus died he prayed, "Father, I have glorified you here on earth and I have finished the work you gave me to do" (Jn 17:4). This is what we want to be able to say at the end of our lives - all has been for the glory of God. We have been faithful to the work of evangelising which the Lord has given us. As Pope Francis says,

> This is our definitive, deepest and greatest motivation, the ultimate reason and meaning behind all we do: the glory of the Father which Jesus sought at every moment of his life.[176]

When Paul was making his way to Jerusalem he received many prophecies that things would not go well for him there. He would face imprisonment and persecution. When speaking to the elders at Ephesus he acknowledged the dangers, but added, "Life to me is not a thing to waste words on, provided that when I finish my race I have carried out the mission the Lord Jesus gave me – and that was to bear witness to the good news of God's grace" (Acts 20:24). This is what matters; that we are faithful to what the Lord has asked of us; that in season and out of season we make the proclamation of the good news of Jesus our life's work (cf 2Tim 4:5).

After his resurrection Jesus commissioned his disciples: "As the Father has sent me so I am sending you" (Jn 20:21). Jesus was constantly aware that "his food" was to do the Father's will in bringing salvation to all (cf Jn 4:34). This is our "food" as well. It is what energises and sustains us. Our life's work is the salvation of others.

We are not to enter heaven alone, but to draw many with us. This is the sign of a fruitful life (cf Jn 15:8). This is the way we give glory to God. At the end of our pilgrim journey we want to be able to say with Jesus, "Father, I have glorified you here on earth and I have finished the work you gave me to do".

Endnotes

[1] Pope Paul VI, *Evangelii Nuntiandi* (EN), 14.
[2] EN, 75.
[3] EN, 27.
[4] Pope John Paul II, *Redemptoris Missio*, (RM), 46.
[5] Pope Benedict XVI, *Deus Caritas Est*, (DCE), 217.
[6] Pope Francis, *Evangelii Gaudium*, (EG) 35.
[7] EG, 36.
[8] Council of Latin American Bishops, *Aparecida Document*, 12.
[9] *Aparecida*, 14.
[10] Address to Bishops of Latin America (*L'Osservatore Romano*, English language edition, 21 October 1992).
[11] RM, 33.
[12] Pope Benedict XVI, Homily at Vespers for St Peter and Paul, 28 June 2010.
[13] Vitterio Messori, *The Ratzinger Report*, (San Francisco: Ignatius, 1985) 43.
[14] Pope John Paul II, *Novo Millenio Ineunte*, (NMI), 40.
[15] EG, 120.
[16] EG, 121.
[17] Origen, *Contra Celsum*, 3, 55, trans Henry Chadwick,(Cambridge University Press: Cambridge, 1953) 165-166.
[18] Pope John Paul II, *Christifidelis Laici*, (CL), 33.
[19] EN, 14.
[20] EG, 24.
[21] NMI, 40.
[22] Pope John XXIII, Apostolic Constitution, *Humanae Saluti*, 25 December 1961, convoking the Second Vatican Council for some time in 1062.
[23] Pope John Paul II, Address to Ecclesial movements and new Communities, St Peters Square, 30 May 1998.

[24] Pope Benedict XVI, Audience, 2005.

[25] Pope John Paul II, Address to a Delegation of members of the Renewal in the Holy Spirit Movement, Rome, 14 March, 2002.

[26] Pope Francis, Address to the Catholic Charismatic Renewal, Olympic Stadium, Rome, 2014.

[27] Pope Francis, Address to the Renewal in the Holy Spirit movement, 3 July 2015.

[28] Pope Francis, Address to the Worldwide Priests Retreat, St John Lateran Basilica, 12 June 2015.

[29] Austen Ivereigh, *The Great Reformer*, (N.Y: Henry Holt and Co., 2014) 291.

[30] Ibid.

[31] In sacramental theology the *"opus operatum"* is the work accomplished. It speaks of the efficacy of the sacraments by the divine action, as long as they are celebrated validly. The *"opus operantis"* is the work yet to be accomplished through the recipients affirmation and cooperation. If the latter is not present the sacrament is valid, but cannot bear fruit in our lives. As children are growing in faith response to the word they are appropriating the gift of baptism and confirmation, but there can be a decisive moment as an adult when the grace of the sacraments becomes released more fully. For many Catholics who have drifted away from the faith and are drawn back to hear the word of God and be renewed in their faith, receiving the baptism in the Spirit can be a decisive time of renewal in all that they received in baptism and confirmation.

[32] Quoted by Raniero Cantalamessa, "Why Baptism in the Spirit is a gift for the Whole Church", given at Conference entitled Awakening the Domestic Church, at Norfolk, Virginia, June 2017. My exposition of baptism in the Spirit draws upon this and other articles of Cantalamessa.

[33] Pope Francis, Vigil of Pentecost and Ecumenical Prayer with Pope Francis at the Circus Maximus on the occasion of the Golden Jubilee of Catholic Charismatic Renewal, 3 June 2017.

[34] EG, 246.

[35] Pope John Paul II, *Ut Unum Sint*, 47-48.

[36] EG, 246.

[37] Address to new ecclesial movements and new communities, St Peters Square, 30 May 1998.

[38] Second Vatican Council, *Lumen Gentium*, 12.

[39] The Siena Institute has done much to help people identify and use their charisms in the life of the Church. The popular "Called and Gifted" program is a great help.

[40] Mary Healy, Discernment and Accompaniment of charisms, in Charisms and the Catholic Church, in *Charisms and the Charismatic Renewal in the Catholic Church* (Colloqium Rome 3-6 April 2008), (ICCRS, Vatican city, 2015) 67.

[41] Hilary Poitiers, *On the Trinity*, 2, 35.

[42] Hilary Poitiers, *Tract on the Psalms*, 64, 14-15.

[43] Cyril of Jerusalem, *Catechetical Lectures*, 18, 32.

[44] See Bruce Yocum, *Prophecy*, Ann Arbor, Michigan, Servant Books, 1976 and Graham Cooke, *Approaching the Heart of Prophecy*, Vacaville: Brilliant Book House, 2006.

[45] Mary Healy, op. cit., 72-73.

[46] Cyprian of Carthage, *Treatise to Donatus on the Grace of God*, 5.

[47] Hilary of Poitiers, *Tract on the Psalms*, 64: 14-15.

[48] Irenaeus, *Against the Heresies* V, 6, 1.

[49] Ibid., 2.32.4

[50] Quoted in Rod Dreher, *The Benedict Option*, (NY: Penguin, 2017) 16-17.

[51] Ibid.

[52] Ibid., 44.

[53] Tracey Rowland, Christ, Culture and the New Evangelisation, in *The New Evangelisation: Faith, People, Context and Practice*, ed. Paul Grogan and Kirsteen Kim, (N.Y. Bloomsbury, 2016) 56-57.

[54] Ibid., 221.

[55] Audience of Pope John Paul II with the ICCRRO Council, Rome, 14 March 1992.

[56] Private audience of Pope John Paul II with the ICCRO Council, Rome, 11 December 1979.

[57] *Faith and Belief in Australia*, McCrindle Research Pty Ltd, Sydney: Baulkham Hills, 2017, 19.

[58] Tracey Rowland, op. cit., 57-59.

[59] Joseph Cardinal Ratzinger with Vitterio Messori, *The Ratzinger Report*, (San Francisco: Ignatius Press, 1985) 53.

[60] See Avery Cardinal Dulles, SJ, Current Theological Obstacles to Evangelisation, in *The New Evangelisation*, edited by Steven Boguslawski and Ralph Martin, (NY: Paulist Press, 2008) 13-25

[61] *Faith and Belief in Australia*, McCrindle Research Pty Ltd, Sydney: Baulkham Hills, 2017.

[62] Ibid., 37-38.

[63] EN, 41.

[64] Ibid., 26.

[65] Reply of Pope Francis to a question by the author at the Third World-Wide Priests Retreat, Basilica of John Lateran, 12 June 2015.

[66] Quoted in Scott Hahn, *Evangelising Catholics*, (Huntington Indiana: Our Sunday Visitor, 2014) 81-82.

[67] Much of this section is inspired by Scott Hahn, *Evangelising Catholics*. Hahn relies upon a sociological study of early Christianity: Rodney Stark, *The Rise of Christianity* (San Francisco: Harper, 1997).

[68] RM, 22.

[69] Quoted in *The Ratzinger Report* (Ignatius: San Francisco, 1985) 43.

[70] Pope John Paul II, Message to Young People on the Occasion of World Youth Day 2000, Rome.

[71] Raniero Cantalamessa, *Come Creator Spirit* (Collegeville Minnesota: Liturgical Press, 2003) 363-365.

[72] EG, 3.

[73] EN, 4.

[74] Fr Ken Barker, *Amazing Love* (Ballan: Connor Court, 2012).

[75] EG, 164.

[76] This is the theme of a book by Jonathan Doyle, *Tools & Fuels: How Catholic*

Teachers can become Saints, Beat Burnout and Save the World (Tuggeranong: Choicez Media, 2017) 52-59.

[77] EN, 18.

[78] RM, 46.

[79] *Catechism of the Catholic Church* (CCC), 1431.

[80] Ibid., 1432.

[81] RM, 47.

[82] For a good introduction to the spiritual life see: Fr Ken Barker, *Becoming Fire* (Balwyn: Freedom Press, 2001).

[83] Pope Benedict, *Sacramentum Caritatis*, 84.

[84] Pope John Paul II, *Ecclesia de Eucharistia*, 22.

[85] Pope Benedict, *Sacramentum Caritatis*, 86.

[86] See Fr Ken Barker, Preaching the Relevance of Christ for Humanity Today, in *The New Evangelisation*, ed. Bishop Julian Porteous, (Ballan: Connor Court, 2008) 103-116.

[87] Ibid., 103-106.

[88] Fr Ken Barker, A Radical Call to Conversion, in *The New Evangelisation*, ed. Bishop Julian Porteous, op. cit., 53-57.

[89] Anthony of Padua, Sermon, found in *Office of Readings*, 13 June.

[90] Fr Ken Barker, A Radical Call to Conversion, op. cit., 57-61.

[91] Ibid., 66-67.

[92] Ibid., 61-64.

[93] Fr Ken Barker, Preaching the Relevance of Christ for Humanity today, op. cit., 111-114.

[94] Quoted in Hans Urs von Balthasar, *The Glory of the Lord*, Vol 1, (New York, Continuum International Publishing Group, 1982).

[95] Fr Anthony Robbie, The Tradition of Lay Preaching, in *The New Evangelisation*, ed. Bishop Julian Porteous, op. cit., 72.

[96] Ibid., 74-76.

[97] See Shayne Bennet, The Phenomenon of Lay Preaching in the Ecclesial Move-

ments and New Communities, in *The New Evangelisation*, ed. Bishop Julian Porteous, op. cit. 90-101.

[98] See Mary Healy, *Healing*, Huntington Indiana: Our Sunday Visitor, 2015.

[99] Pope Benedict VI, *Jesus of Nazareth*, (N.Y.: Doubleday, 2007) 176.

[100] Justin Martyr, *Second Apology*, 6, 5-6.

[101] Origen, *Against Celsus*, 7.4.

[102] Augustine, *Retractions*, 426-428.

[103] Augustine, *The City of God*, XXII, 8.

[104] See Fr Ken Barker, *The Wonder of the Eucharist*, (Ballarat: Connor Court, 2015): 119-125.

[105] For a good introduction Richard McAlear, *The Power of Healing Prayer*, Huntington Indiana: Our Sunday Visitor, 2012.

[106] See Fr Ken Barker, *His Name is Mercy*, (Ballan: Connor Court,

[107] A good introduction is Neal Lozano, *Resisting the Devil: A Catholic Perspective on Deliverance*, Huntington Indiana: Our Sunday Visitor, 2009.

[108] The steps here are outlined in Neal Lozano, *Unbound: a Practical Guide to Deliverance*, Grand Rapids, Michigan: Chosen Books, 2010.

[109] Fr James Mallon, *Divine Renovation*, (Mulgrave: Garratt Publishing, 2014) 141.

[110] EG, 165.

[111] EG, 114.

[112] EG, 27.

[113] EG, 24.

[114] EG, 22; *Aparecida*, 201.

[115] EG, 49.

[116] This is the strategy proposed in Rod Dreher, *The Benedict Option*, (NY: Penguin, 2017) 2.

[117] Pope John Paul II, Address to Young People, Vigil WYD, Downsview Park Toronto, 27 July 2002.

[118] See Fr Ken Barker, *Religious Education, Catechesis and Freedom*, (Birmingham Alabama: Religious Education Press, 1981) 163.

[119] James Mallon, op. cit., 91.
[120] Attributed to Peter Drucker and made famous by Mark Fields, President of Ford.
[121] EG, 169.
[122] Sherry Weddel, *Forming Intentional Disciples*, (Huntington Indiana: Our Sunday Visitor, 2012) 81.
[123] EG, 48.
[124] EG, 49.
[125] EG, 197.
[126] EG, 198.
[127] EN, 31-35.
[128] St John Chrysostom, *Homily on Lazarus*, 2, 5.
[129] Gregory the Great. *Pastoral Rule*, 3, 21.
[130] EG, 201.
[131] EG, 188.
[132] RM, 59.
[133] EG, 191.
[134] Holy See Press Office, Message of the Holy Father to the Executive President of World Economic Forum on the occasion of the Annual meeting at Davos, Switzerland, 20 January 2016.
[135] EG, 200.
[136] Ibid.
[137] EG, 49.
[138] Pope Benedict XVI, World Communication Day Message, 2013.
[139] Fr Robert Barron, "The Virtual Areopagus" in Brandon Vogt, *The Church and New Media: Blogging Converts, Online Activists, and Bishops who Tweet* (Huntington Indiana: Our Sunday visitor, 2011), 29.
[140] Ibid., 27.
[141] Pope Francis, Address to Pontifical Council for Social Communication, 2013.
[142] Pope Francis, World Communication Day Message, 2014.

[143] Pope John Paul II, Letter to Artists, read at meeting in Sistine Chapel, 21 November 2009, 16.

[144] Feodor Dostoyevsky, *The Idiot*, Part III, ch. 5.

[145] Peter Kreeft, and R.K. Tacelli, *Handbook of Catholic Apologetics: Reasoned Answers to Questions of Faith* (San Francisco: Ignatius Press, 2009), 87.

[146] Pope John Paul II, Letter to Artists, read at meeting in Sistine Chapel, 4 April 1999.

[147] Pope Benedict XVI, Address to Meeting with Artists, Sistine Chapel, 21 November 2009.

[148] St Augustine, *Confessions*, Bk IV, 13.20.

[149] Synod on New Evangelisation, 2012, Proposition of Bishops, 20.

[150] EN, 20.

[151] Pope Francis, Interview with *Asia Times*, 2 February 2016.

[152] Pope John Paul II, *Ecclesia Oceania*, 16.

[153] Ibid.

[154] Ibid.

[155] Ibid., 17

[156] Pope John Paul II, Address to Aboriginal People and Torres Strait Islanders, Alice Springs, November 1986, 12.

[157] Ibid.

[158] Ibid., 13.

[159] Cyril John, *Pray Lifting up Holy Hands*, (New Delhi: ICCRS, 2012) 17-18

[160] Ibid., 21-28.

[161] Anne Marie Gatenby, *A Practical Guide to Intercession*, (Keilor East: Comsoda Communications, 2015) 9-11.

[162] Therese of Lisieux, *Story of a Soul*, (Washington DC: ICS Publications, 1972) 254.

[163] Catherine of Siena, Letter 296 to Don Giovanni of the Cells.

[164] EN, 24.

[165] EN, 74-75.

[166] EG, 280.
[167] RM, 45.
[168] EG, 266.
[169] EG, 88.
[170] EG, 91.
[171] Ibid.
[172] EG, 273.
[173] EG, 270.
[174] NMI,
[175] EG, 85.
[176] EG, 267.

www.ingramcontent.com/pod-product-compliance
Lightning Source LLC
Chambersburg PA
CBHW071843230426
43671CB00012B/2049